FABER has published children's ~~graphic books~~ books since 1929. T. S. Eliot's *Old Possum's Book of Practical Cats* and Ted Hughes's *The Iron Man* were among the first. Our catalogue at the time said that 'it is by reading such books that children learn the difference between the shoddy and the genuine'. We still believe in the power of reading to transform children's lives. All our books are chosen with the express intention of growing a love of reading, a thirst for knowledge ~~and to motivate~~ and to cultivate empathy. We pride ourselves on responsible editing. Last but not least, we believe in kind and inclusive books in which all children feel represented and important.

David Long

Writer and historian David Long is the ~~award-winning~~ award-winning and bestselling author of the acclaimed Survivors series, *Pirates Magnified, We are the Romans, The World's Most Magnificent Machines,* ~~Tragedy at Sea,~~ *Tragedy at Sea, The Story of the London Underground* and more than twenty other non-fiction books on a wide range of historical subjects. He lives in Suffolk and has two teenage sons.

Terri Po is a children's book illustrator who was highly commended in the FAB Prize. ~~She originally~~ She is originally from Hong Kong but graduated from the University of Edinburgh in 2018. ~~She~~ She creates editorial illustrations, ~~infographics and~~ infographics and illustrated books, as well as doing live graphic facilitation.

Terri Po

DAVID LONG

Illustrated by
TERRI PO

SPIES

The most thrilling spy stories from around the world . . .

faber

First published ▮▮▮▮▮▮ in the UK in 2022
First published in the US in 2022
by Faber & Faber Limited
Bloomsbury House, 74–77 Great Russell Street
London, WC1B 3DA
faberchildrens.co.uk

▮▮▮▮▮▮▮▮

Typeset by Faber in Mr Eaves
This font has been specially chosen to support reading

Printed and bound in Latvia

▮▮▮▮▮▮▮▮▮▮▮▮▮▮▮▮▮▮

The right of David Long and Terri Po to be identified as author and illustrator respectively
of this work has been asserted in accordance with Section 77 of the Copyright,
Designs and Patents Act 1988

▮▮▮▮▮▮▮▮▮▮▮

A CIP record for this book is available from the British Library

▮▮▮▮▮▮▮▮▮▮▮▮

ISBN 978–0–571–36184–7

2 4 6 8 10 9 7 5 3 1

For Hugo and Ivo

Great-nephews of Air Chief Marshal Sir Lewis Hodges

KCB, CBE, DSO & Bar, DFC & Bar,

DL

SPIES

CONTENTS

Introduction

Spies and secret agents have been hard at work for centuries, risking their lives, and sometimes changing the course of history. More than four hundred years ago England's royal spymaster, Sir Francis Walsingham, discovered a plot to remove Elizabeth I from the throne, and in the American War of Independence in the eighteenth century one of the most brilliant agents was an African American slave called James Armistead Lafayette.

Most countries today have spies working undercover, although very few admit it. The work they do can be exciting and often highly dangerous, but rarely as glamorous as it appears on television and in films.

However, it is in wartime that spies and their secret organisations have become most notorious, playing an important part in discovering battle plans and disrupting an enemy's ability to fight. Knowing about an attack in advance, or the details of a deadly new weapon, can completely alter the outcome of a battle. A single spy can save thousands of lives in this way, although if a secret gets into the wrong hands the outcome can be disastrous, resulting in death and destruction.

People become spies for various reasons.

Some do it for money or are tricked into it without realising. It might be for love of their own country, or out of fear and hatred of another one. Others do it in an effort to save innocent lives, although many courageous men and women have died this way, often in horrific circumstances.

Because of this, it can be hard to judge whether a spy is good or bad (it depends which side you're on), but when their stories include so much courage, ingenuity and determination it is impossible not to be impressed by their actions and daring.

Spying goes on all the time, but some of the most astonishing spy stories relate to wartime, in particular the Second World War, when so many men and women risked their lives this way. Their work was so secret that some of the details have not yet been revealed, but their adventures still sound mind-boggling after all these years.

Giliana Gerson

Making Friends in All the Right Places

When France was invaded by Nazi Germany during the Second World War, thousands of courageous men and women known as freedom fighters or partisans joined the French Resistance. This was a secret army which spent the next four years attacking factories and other buildings that were being used by the enemy as prisons and for storing weapons. As well as sabotaging airfields, bridges and railways across France, its members stole top-secret plans and kidnapped collaborators, which is what they called those French people who helped the Germans.

This work was vitally important, but extremely dangerous for everyone involved. The activities of the Resistance infuriated the Germans, and many members of the organisation were hunted down and imprisoned. Some were tortured and even killed for refusing to betray their comrades or to give away details of any missions they were planning.

These men and women were mostly volunteers, not professional soldiers. Even schoolchildren sometimes became involved. For example, two French schoolgirls secretly drained the oil from several enemy vehicles one night, and replaced it with contaminated oil which wrecked the engines.

Because **this sort of work was so important**, the British created their own secret organisation to help France and other occupied countries in their struggle against the enemy. This was called the Special Operations Executive or SOE. The prime minister, Winston Churchill, said he wanted to 'set Europe ablaze' by making life as hard as possible for the invading Germans. He ordered the SOE to send secret agents, guns, money and explosives to partisans fighting in all the different countries which had been overrun by the German army.

The SOE's first agent to cross to France was Georges Bégué, a French engineer who lived in England, had an English wife, and spoke both English and French very well. Under cover of darkness he was parachuted into France with a powerful radio transmitter hidden in his suitcase. He used this

to communicate with the SOE's London headquarters while he helped the partisans organise themselves into a more effective fighting force.

Women had several advantages over men when it came to spying, although it took a while for Churchill to understand what these were. It took him even longer to agree to send female spies overseas, but eventually more than 3,200 women joined the SOE.

Some were young girls who had just finished school. Others were older, ranging from working-class women to aristocrats. Incredibly, they were the only women in any British or American organisation to be issued with weapons during the whole of the Second World War (1939–45).

As spies, they had to be brave, quick-thinking and exceptionally calm under pressure: twenty-year-old Anne-Marie Walters, for example, carried on with her mission despite being injured in a plane crash when she first took off for France.

Because so many men were away fighting in the war, female spies were able to blend in more easily in towns and cities where women and children made up most of the population. They had another important advantage too: at least to begin with, it hadn't even occurred to the German authorities to start looking for female spies. Soldiers, sailors and pilots were nearly all men, so

very few people guessed that an ordinary-looking young woman could be working as a spy.

Georges Bégué didn't know it but Britain's **first female spy** was already in France. Giliana Gerson had been born in Chile and lived in Paris, where she worked as an actress. Her South American passport meant she could travel around the country quite easily, which British people couldn't do. She used her training as an actress to make it look as though she wasn't an agent at all but just a tourist.

Gerson spent around a month pretending she was enjoying her French holiday, but really she was making friends with many of the people she met in bars and cafes. She spoke several languages fluently and was trying to find out which people she could trust and who were traitors working for the Germans. It was very risky. No one would admit to a complete stranger that he or she was a partisan, and if Gerson had told the wrong person what she was doing she would have been arrested immediately.

Gerson wanted to set up a network of trustworthy French individuals who might be useful to the SOE. This meant identifying people in the Resistance who could be counted on to help spies arriving from London. They could also assist Royal Air Force (RAF) pilots who had been shot down over France and needed to get back to Britain.

By 1941 more and more secret agents were being sent from Britain to France. They usually arrived at night by aeroplane or submarine. Both were hazardous ways to travel in wartime. Aircraft flying across the English Channel were frequently shot down, and many agents were injured after making a jump in the dark. Others were arrested the moment they landed because the enemy heard the aircraft coming. Submarines were also risky because the German navy had so many more of them than the British had.

Once landed, the **agents needed a lot of support** to survive in France. The same was true for RAF pilots who had been shot down. Even if they survived the crash, or a parachute jump made in total darkness, it was impossible to last very long behind enemy lines without food and shelter. They could only get this from people living in the local towns and villages.

Similarly, if a pilot was injured in a crash, he couldn't visit a hospital or see a doctor without the Germans finding out. Gerson worked hard to identify people she could trust to look after them and treat their injuries. Fortunately, this was something she was very good at.

As long as the Germans were in control, even ordinary French citizens had to carry identity papers showing who they were and where they lived, and giving them permission to travel around. The enemy had military and police

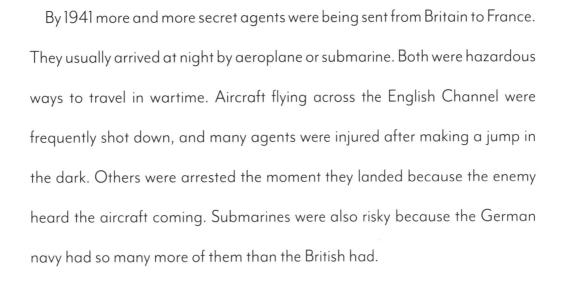

checkpoints all over France to trap spies and saboteurs, and Gerson knew that anyone who didn't have the necessary documents would be arrested and possibly even shot.

To prevent this happening to any SOE agents, she spent much of her imaginary holiday stealing or borrowing as many official identity documents as she could carry. She smuggled dozens of these back to Britain so they could be copied by the SOE's special forgery department. This was based at a large country house near Harlow in Essex and had the code name 'Station XIV'. Hidden in its cellars, a small team of expert forgers worked to produce more than 275,000 fake passports, ration cards and foreign banknotes for agents to take with them on their missions.

Gerson had another skill too **`an incredible memory`** for faces and tiny details. During her stay in France she memorised an amazing amount of information that she thought might be useful to the SOE. This included train and bus timetables, which agents needed to learn to avoid detection, and details about the dangers they might face in particular areas. She even worked out a secret route spies could use to get from one part of France to another without being stopped and questioned.

Like the forged documents based on those she smuggled back, this information was crucial for the agents who followed Giliana Gerson into

France. We don't know exactly how many agents she helped in this way, but it is known that many spies avoided capture by following her advice. Similarly, hundreds of RAF pilots were able to get back home using the sort of escape routes that Gerson helped to plan and organise. Thanks to Giliana Gerson they could rejoin their squadrons and continue fighting the enemy.

Roald Dahl

From Spy to Storyteller

Long before he began writing stories about witches, Twits and magical chocolate factories, Roald Dahl was a Royal Air Force pilot and then a spy.

Dahl's flying career had got off to a bad start when he crashed his first aeroplane in the Libyan desert in 1940. He later boasted about how the Gloster Gladiator biplane had been shot down by the enemy, but in fact it simply ran out of fuel after the young, inexperienced pilot lost his way. His attempt to land the aircraft as gently as possible also went wrong when one of the wheels hit a rock and the spinning propeller ploughed violently into the ground.

The impact fractured Dahl's skull and broke his nose, and he was knocked unconscious for several seconds. Luckily, when he came to, he managed to climb out of the cockpit before the burning Gladiator exploded. Dahl was dazed, but dragged himself away from the wreckage as quickly as he could. Moments later the ground around him was showered with razor-sharp metal shards and hundreds of rounds of deadly ammunition which had been unleashed by the heat.

Dahl was temporarily blinded in the accident and his recovery was so slow that it took more than six months before he was given the go-ahead to fly again. Unfortunately, a few weeks after his first genuine combat mission (over Greece) he admitted he was still suffering from blinding headaches and blackouts. He was immediately banned from flying military aircraft and sent back to Britain.

Dahl had loved being a pilot, but his next assignment was what he considered an unimportant desk job. He was employed at the British Embassy in Washington, although he was also asked to give a series of talks to American audiences about his time in the RAF. The US hadn't yet joined the war and Britain was desperate to ensure that it came in on the right side. It was hoped that if American politicians heard about the experiences of a young, wounded pilot they might be persuaded to send troops to fight alongside Britain.

The British had been exploring different ways of convincing the US to join the war for some time. Although the American president, Franklin D. Roosevelt, was fiercely opposed to Germany's Nazi government and its Japanese allies, any efforts at persuasion had to be carried out in complete secrecy. This was because millions of Americans didn't agree with their president. They didn't want to risk soldiers' lives in a war that was being fought thousands of miles away in countries most of them had never even visited.

As part of **this secret campaign**, Dahl was asked to join an organisation called British Security Coordination (BSC). This had been set up by Britain's Secret Intelligence Service (known as MI6) as a way to supply pro-British and anti-German stories to American newspapers and television stations. Hundreds of agents were employed spreading propaganda in this way. They were also ordered to spy on Americans to find out whether they were more likely to support Britain or her enemies, and to commit small, hostile acts against any who were thought to be pro-German. These included putting dead rats in the water tanks of their homes and letting the air out of their car tyres.

Most of the agents concentrated on ordinary Americans, but Dahl was brought in to spy on the country's most senior politicians and some of its richest businessmen. After being invited to spend a weekend in New York with

the president himself, he wrote a ten-page report for the British prime minister to read. His report warned Winston Churchill that both Roosevelt and his vice president wished Britain to win the war, but that they hated the British Empire and wanted every country in it to free itself of British rule after the war. Dahl also reported that the president had a secret girlfriend, a Norwegian princess, although this turned out not to be true.

Another of his important contacts was a rich newspaper owner who allowed Dahl to see confidential documents belonging to the vice president. These contained secret details about American aircraft manufacturers and their plans for the future, which Dahl, as a former pilot, found fascinating. He could see that they would be useful to the RAF and, without his contact realising it, arranged for a colleague to come and copy the documents. The information was then sent back to London.

Dahl was also involved in **an elaborate scheme** to persuade Americans that Hitler planned to take over South America. This involved a stolen map which showed different regions of the continent each under the control of a *Gauleiter* or German official. The map was almost certainly a British-made forgery, but President Roosevelt used it to warn American citizens that Germany had plans which affected not just South America but the United States itself.

At the end of 1941 the US finally declared war on Germany and Japan after the Japanese bombed its naval base at Pearl Harbor. The BSC office in New York was quietly closed because MI6 and the British government didn't want Americans finding out that they had been spied on, lied to and tricked. This meant that Dahl and his fellow agents were no longer needed.

It had been **an exciting time for Dahl** – maybe even as exciting as flying over the desert – and, interestingly, it was while he was employed as a spy that he took his first steps towards becoming an author. This happened when a journalist arrived in Washington to interview him about his time in the RAF. He asked Dahl to let him have some notes about his plane crash and when he saw what Dahl had written (including the lie about being shot down) he was so impressed that he arranged for it to be published in an American magazine.

This was the first thing that Roald Dahl had ever written for publication. He went on to sell more than 250 million books, including *The BFG* and *Charlie and the Chocolate Factory*, as well as writing scripts for films such as the James Bond adventure *You Only Live Twice.*

Virginia Hall

Spying, Subversion and Sabotage

Virginia Hall was only twenty-seven when she accidentally shot herself in the leg while on holiday in Turkey in 1933. Her leg wouldn't heal and it had to be amputated from the knee. Following the operation, Hall was fitted with a wooden leg, which she nicknamed 'Cuthbert', and a metal foot.

Because of this serious injury, the young American was refused a job with the US Foreign Office. Instead she volunteered to drive an ambulance for the French army at the start of the war. Her work involved rescuing wounded soldiers from the battlefield, as aircraft flew low overhead and attacked the ambulances with machine guns and bombs. It was a dangerous job for anyone, but Hall's heavy wooden leg made it difficult for her to move around and it put her in even greater peril. When the French surrendered, she managed to escape back to England and accepted a less adventurous job in the American Embassy in London.

After a few months of boring office life, Hall was approached by someone from the SOE who could see that this determined and hardworking young woman might make a good agent. Hall already spoke French, German and Italian and she could understand Russian. She also knew her way around France and after eight months' training she went back there to live and work as a spy.

The US had not yet joined the war against Germany in April 1941, but spying was still dangerous for American citizens. Hall was given false identity papers and told to pose as a reporter for the *New York Post* newspaper. She spent more than a year doing this, while in reality she was part of a small group of agents (called a circuit) which was based between the cities of Toulouse and Lyons.

Hall's circuit helped other SOE agents who were arriving in France. Its members also gathered useful information about the enemy, which they sent back to London in coded messages. These included the locations of German troops and their ammunition and fuel stores. She also provided details of a

secret submarine base which was later bombed in a daring raid.

One of the SOE's most important jobs at this time was to supply members of the French Resistance with money. On one occasion, a newly arrived agent called Peter Churchill managed to smuggle thousands of banknotes into France. Hall introduced him to a Resistance leader so that he could hand the money over.

Afterwards she helped Churchill to escape over the mountains into Spain, which was the best way to get back to England, to prepare for another mission. Hall knew that a single man travelling on his own would attract the attention of the Gestapo, the German secret police, so she went with Churchill to make it look as if they were a married couple.

The trick worked and eventually `he made it home safely`. Unfortunately, by the time Hall returned to welcome the next agent arriving in France (a radio operator who came by submarine), members of the Gestapo had become suspicious about the woman they called 'the limping lady'.

It wasn't long before her name appeared on a list of people that the Gestapo chief Klaus Barbie wanted to arrest and interrogate. Barbie had a terrible reputation. He was nicknamed 'the Butcher' because he tortured many of his prisoners, and historians now think he was responsible for around fourteen thousand deaths. Hall realised she had to get out of France as quickly as possible.

Before heading back to the Spanish border, she sent a radio message to England explaining what she was about to do. When she said she hoped 'Cuthbert' wouldn't cause her any problems in the mountains, she was told to kill him by a radio operator, who didn't realise she was talking about her wooden leg.

Spain was ruled by a fascist dictator called General Franco, but it was still a much safer place than France. However, getting there involved a long journey which was tough even for somebody with two legs. The highest peaks in the Pyrenees are more than 3,400 metres high and, with winter closing in, deep snow and ice made it harder than ever to travel through the remote and mountainous countryside.

Hall spent two days and two nights in the mountains, trekking along steep, rock-strewn paths to a height of around 2,200 metres and travelling more than eighty kilometres – all of it on foot. The Pyrenees cover over 190,000 square kilometres and without a specialist guide it is incredibly easy to get lost even in daylight. Hall was able to find her way to Spain, but when she got there she was exhausted. Perhaps because she was so cold and tired, she made a careless mistake.

Hall's plan was to make it look as though she was just an ordinary traveller catching a train to the city of Barcelona. However, she got to the station too early – several hours before the train arrived – and a member of staff realised she must have crossed the border illegally. He called the police and she was immediately locked up.

Eventually the US authorities managed to get Hall released and she travelled back to London, but she was determined to return to France as quickly as possible to carry on her work. Everyone knew how good she was at organising agents, supplying them with money and guns, and helping British airmen to escape – but no one at the SOE would give her permission to go. Because the Gestapo knew who she was, and because her name was on Barbie's infamous list, Virginia Hall would have been arrested and probably killed if she went back.

Hall knew this too, but she refused to be put off and announced that she was going to leave the SOE. By this time the US had declared war on Germany and had its own secret organisation, called the Office of Strategic Services (OSS). Hall decided to join this so that she could continue working as a spy.

One night she was dropped by parachute into France. This was dangerous enough for anyone, let alone someone with a wooden leg. Hall decided the best way was to take her false leg off and tuck it into her backpack before jumping out of the aeroplane.

Disguised as a farmhand, Hall landed safely and went on to teach dozens of genuine agricultural workers how to use guns and explosives. They used these to wreck many of the roads and railways the German army needed to maintain its control of France. This made it much easier for Britain and its allies to launch their own invasion (known as D-Day) to free France from Nazi rule in 1944.

When the war ended, Virginia Hall went back home to America. She never spoke about her activities, not even to her family, but she was awarded several medals for her amazing achievements, including the Distinguished Service Cross. She was the only female civilian to receive this prestigious honour during the whole of the Second World War.

Lewis Hodges

Missions by Moonlight

One of the quickest and most effective ways to drop a secret agent behind enemy lines was to use an aeroplane called a Westland Lysander. These were also used to rescue agents and fly them home again at the end of each mission.

The Lysander was a curious, slightly old-fashioned-looking aeroplane. It wasn't sleek or fast like a Spitfire and it couldn't fly very high. Even the newest 'Mk III SD' version didn't have any guns or bombs, and all Lysanders were uncomfortable to fly and extremely noisy.

What the Lysander could do, however, was take off and land really quickly.

It didn't need a long take-off run to gather enough speed to get airborne and it didn't need a concrete runway. Because it was so tough and rugged, it was perfect for landing in a farm field or even a clearing in a forest. Once on the ground, the pilot could quickly turn around and take off again as soon as the agent had scrambled aboard.

The pilots called these agents 'Joes' (regardless of gender) and 'SD' stood for Special Duties, which was the name given to almost three hundred secret Lysander missions. These were mostly carried out to support the SOE and the French Resistance.

Special Duties pilots like young Lewis Hodges were handpicked for these assignments and they were forbidden to tell even their parents what they were doing. Their work was vitally important but also extremely hazardous and for a flight to be successful a pilot needed a lot of luck as well as an extraordinary amount of skill.

Hodges was one of the **most famous Lysander pilots** of all. He had joined the RAF straight from school in London, and he was still only twenty-two when he met his first French Resistance members.

Hodges was flying his badly damaged bomber back from a raid when it crashed in France. The crew were all taken prisoner, but Hodges managed to

escape from his captors and, with help from the Resistance, he made his way out of France. Unfortunately he was arrested again after crossing the border illegally into Spain and it took him nearly a year to get back to England.

Hodges went back to being a bomber pilot and took part in a deadly raid on two important German battleships, the *Scharnhorst* and the *Gneisenau*. Because he was such an outstanding pilot he was then ordered to report to an airfield in Bedfordshire called RAF Tempsford. This was home to the RAF's top secret No. 161 Squadron, which operated Special Duties flights using Lysanders and other aircraft.

From then on, Hodges always **flew alone** if he was rescuing an agent and mostly flew at night to avoid detection. Most of his missions involved flying hundreds of kilometres over enemy territory. Like every Lysander pilot he had to keep an eye open for German night fighters trying to shoot him down, and avoid being hit by the big anti-aircraft guns firing at him from the ground.

Each flight lasted for hours and the Lysander's cabin was cold and noisy. This type of aircraft wasn't fitted with radar or any sophisticated navigation equipment so Hodges could only tell where he was by using a simple paper map, his watch and a compass. Occasionally a full moon illuminated a river or another landmark, but otherwise he had to hold the map in one hand while flying the aircraft using the other.

The maps were folded in a way that made it possible to open them with one hand, and illuminated by a tiny lamp so Hodges could check the aircraft's location during the flight. But even with a full moon it could be extremely difficult to identify the correct small field or forest clearing to land in.

To help Hodges do this, members of **the Resistance** were usually on the ground to guide him in. Back in London the BBC would broadcast coded messages on the radio each evening. An ordinary person listening to the programme would have had no idea these contained secret messages, but the Resistance could tell if a Special Duties flight was coming and where its pilot wanted to land.

After reaching the right part of France, Hodges would have to look out for a torch being flashed up at him from the ground. Once the waiting agents were sure this was the right aircraft, they would mark out a path on the grass using more torches or burning rags. In this way Hodges could be sure he was landing in the right place.

Once down on the ground it was important to turn the aircraft around and take off as quickly as possible. If any German police heard the sound of the noisy Lysander, or saw Hodges landing, they would rush over with all guns blazing. A short metal ladder fitted to the side of the aircraft enabled the agent to climb on board in just a few seconds so that it would take less than

five minutes to land, load and take off again.

Altogether Hodges and his fellow Special Duties pilots carried more than four hundred people this way. For security reasons they rarely knew who the 'Joes' were, but after the war Hodges was made a Commander of the prestigious French Légion d'Honneur. After being given this very special medal he was told that one of his passengers had been Vincent Auriol, France's new president. Later, in old age, Hodges discovered that another of his 'Joes' had been François Mitterrand. He too became president of France and promoted Hodges to the rank of Grand Officer of the Légion.

This was **a huge and unusual honour** because being made a Grand Officer is an exceptionally rare thing, especially for a person who isn't French. Hodges remained in the RAF after the war, eventually becoming an Air Chief Marshal, and in 1968 he was knighted by the Queen.

Noor Inayat Khan

The First Woman Wireless Operator

Working as an SOE agent during the Second World War was so dangerous that nearly a quarter of those who were sent behind enemy lines never came home again.

Wireless operators had one of the most dangerous jobs of all. They used portable radio transmitters to send coded messages and to receive instructions from London. The instructions helped members of the Resistance plan their attacks on the enemy, or told them which bridge or building to blow up next.

Sending **secret messages in code** meant the enemy couldn't understand them, but the Germans had electronic equipment which could easily detect where a radio signal was coming from. They used this information to find where the agents were hiding so they could arrest them and stop them sending any more messages.

At this time, any private individual found using a radio transmitter in France would be arrested and then imprisoned or shot. There were no exceptions to this law: transmitters were completely illegal. This meant the operator had to stay hidden to stay alive, and if he or she needed to move from one building to another, the transmitter needed to be concealed in some way. It might be hidden in a suitcase or under a cover, or even in a bundle of firewood.

Operators were trained to hide out for days in attics, cellars and bombed-out buildings, and to disguise the transmitter's aerial so it couldn't be seen from outside. They took lots of precautions, including disguising the aerial as a washing line and posting someone on the street outside to act as a look-out. But even so, many operators lasted less than six weeks before being discovered, and so the SOE was always looking for new volunteers to train.

Noor Inayat Khan was one of the first female wireless operators, and in June 1943 she became the very first one to be sent to France. She was a

Muslim from an Indian family, although she had been born in Russia and was educated in France. Khan had been a shy, quiet child, but in 1940 she travelled to London because she wanted to help free France and the other countries that had been invaded by Germany. She joined the Women's Auxiliary Air Force (WAAF), but women were not yet allowed to become pilots and she found the work really boring.

Fortunately, members of the WAAF could transfer to the SOE if they had the right skills. Khan spoke French as well as English, she knew her way around Paris, and the WAAF had taught her how to use a radio transmitter. In tests she demonstrated that she could send messages quickly and accurately. A report on her overall performance described her as energetic and enthusiastic, but it also said she wasn't very intelligent.

This wasn't true at all. Khan had been a successful student at two very good universities in Paris. She wrote poetry and composed music, and had already published a book of children's stories. Her skill as a musician (she played the harp beautifully) may even have helped her to tap out messages faster than anyone else.

Knowing all this, the writer of the report still said he thought that Khan didn't really have the brains or the personality needed to work as a spy. Luckily the head of the SOE's French section didn't believe this at all. He just scribbled the word NONSENSE across the front page of the report – and Noor Inayat Khan got the job.

Normally agents **trained for many months** before they were sent overseas. During this time they were taught armed and unarmed combat, map reading, how to disguise themselves and how to use guns and explosives. Because new wireless operators were so badly needed, Khan's vital training was cut short so that she could get to France as soon as possible.

Before leaving, she had the chance to take part in one practice mission. She was also interrogated by the SOE staff pretending to be members of the German Gestapo, which she admitted she found terrifying. She was concerned that her family would be frightened for her and that, because her training was incomplete, she would have to rely heavily on her own intelligence and initiative. Despite these worries, and the fact that as a pacifist she was opposed to the war, Khan knew she had the skills to do something useful to help the troops who were fighting.

Like other SOE recruits, Khan flew to northern France in a tough little Westland Lysander. The flight was even more uncomfortable than usual because she was squashed into the small back seat of the aeroplane with another SOE agent. After a bumpy landing, the two of them jumped out and made contact with members of the French Resistance. Khan's orders were to

join a particular group of agents (known as a 'circuit') with the code name Prosper.

As Prosper's wireless operator her job was to be the link between the circuit and SOE headquarters in London. Sending a message might take Khan less than a minute, but agents often had to wait a long time for a reply, which made it even more dangerous than sending a message. The Germans were becoming very good at detecting radio signals and the longer she had her transmitter switched on, the greater risk there was of being detected and captured.

Khan kept moving around to avoid detection. This was important because there weren't as many Asian people in France in the 1940s as there are today. Khan was disguised as a nurse, but she still looked a bit conspicuous. She also knew that if she was caught, she would have no excuse for having a radio transmitter with her.

Within days of her first message being sent, several members of the Prosper group were arrested. This made Khan's situation even more dangerous because any one of them could have identified her and told the Germans where to find her. The SOE decided to fly Khan back to England as quickly as possible, but she refused to go. The Resistance needed wireless operators like her. Khan also felt that if she stayed in France she could help build a new network of agents to replace those who had been arrested.

Despite this **increased risk**, Khan managed to keep out of sight for several months. She dyed her hair blonde to alter her appearance and at one point she was helping other circuits by doing the work of at least six wireless operators. For a while she was the SOE's only link between Paris and London, and the Germans were desperate to find out who was sending all these messages. They only discovered who it was because another agent turned traitor and led the Germans to Noor Inayat Khan. This may have been because a large sum of money was paid to the traitor as a bribe.

Khan was arrested and taken to Paris, and questioned by the secret police. She tried to escape but failed, and then made another attempt during an air raid. While everyone in the building ran down to the cellars to escape from the bombs, Khan climbed onto the roof and attempted to clamber over to the building next door. Unfortunately, she didn't get very far before her captors realised she was missing and brought her back.

Because Khan refused to sign a document saying she wouldn't try to escape again, she was taken to Germany in handcuffs and locked in a prison cell on her own. For the next few months she was kept in chains. She was beaten and interrogated repeatedly. Other prisoners could hear her crying at night, but she refused to give away any secrets.

Her courage and determination impressed her captors, but they also knew

an agent as good as Khan was highly dangerous. Eventually the Germans realised they weren't going to get anything from her and on 12 September 1944 Noor Inayat Khan was taken from the prison and shot. Witnesses later said that her last word was 'Liberté' – the French for freedom.

Khan's **quiet heroism** and her incredible determination have never been forgotten. After the war she was posthumously awarded the George Cross (Britain's highest civilian award) for displaying 'the most conspicuous courage, both moral and physical, over a period of more than twelve months'. In 2014 British members of the public donated more than £100,000 for a memorial sculpture of Khan to be put up in a square in central London.

Witold Pilecki

Breaking into a Death Camp

In the 1930s and 40s, as well as waging war across Europe and North Africa, the Nazi government in Germany ordered the arrest and murder of millions of ordinary men, women and children. A vast network of special prisons called concentration camps was built for this purpose. The first ones were in Germany, but others were built in the countries Germany invaded as the war went on. The inmates of these camps included Roma and Sinti people, gay men, disabled people, Jehovah's Witnesses, and political opponents of the Nazis such as communists. By far the largest group, however, were Jews.

The biggest of the camps was Auschwitz in Poland. To begin with it looked like any other prisoner-of-war camp, but eventually it grew to house tens of thousands of inmates in wooden barracks or huts, surrounded by high, electrified barbed-wire fences. They were guarded by soldiers in tall watchtowers who had machine guns and powerful searchlights.

Local people were forbidden to go anywhere near the camp, so for a while nobody knew exactly what went on inside. However, members of the Polish underground or resistance were becoming suspicious. The camp was growing larger and larger, but with trains bringing prisoners from all over Europe it was obvious that there would never be enough wooden huts to house them all. Soon they realised that more people were arriving at the camp than were imprisoned there. What had happened to everyone else?

Many Poles didn't know it yet, but many of the prisoners being sent to Auschwitz were Jewish families. The Nazis had already introduced laws making it impossible for them to live and work in Germany. This was the beginning of a terrible period of history called the Holocaust or *Shoah*. Soon they began forcing Jews out of other European countries as well, as these came under German control.

These Jews were ordinary men, women and children. They weren't charged with any crime or tried in court. Whole families were arrested simply for being Jewish. After being robbed of all their possessions, they were forced onto

trains going to Auschwitz and numerous other, smaller camps. Instead of railway carriages, the prisoners were locked inside trucks that were designed for transporting cattle.

Witold Pilecki was a captain in the Polish army. He had gone into hiding when his country was invaded, and began organising a resistance group. He and his comrades wanted to find out what was going on at Auschwitz, so they hatched a daring plan for one of them to get inside the camp. Once in, they thought, the agent could smuggle information out about what was happening inside and maybe even organise a break-out.

Pilecki was asked if he would consider going into the camp and, very bravely, he agreed to try. He was issued with false identity papers in September 1940 (naming him as Tomasz Serafiński) and shortly afterwards he managed to get arrested by the Gestapo. Two days later 'Tomasz' was sent to Auschwitz.

He arrived with **more than a hundred** other prisoners and was immediately horrified. As soon as they jumped down from the train, teams of armed guards began beating them with heavy clubs. Nearly a dozen prisoners were pulled out of the crowd, apparently at random, and shot dead. Another man was beaten to death on the spot after saying he was a doctor. The same thing happened to several others, all of whom were Jewish.

Stunned by the violence and the brutality of the guards, Pilecki was led away to be stripped and searched for any valuables. After this he and the other men had their heads shaved and were given identity numbers and prison clothes, which were striped like pyjamas. Minutes later, one of the German guards told them, 'Let none of you imagine that he will ever leave this place alive.'

Auschwitz was clearly `not just a prison camp`. The same guard explained that food in the camp was strictly rationed and that no one would receive enough of it to survive for more than a few weeks. Another guard joked about how the only way out of the camp was up the chimney, meaning that when the prisoners were dead their bodies would be burned to smoke and ash in its enormous incinerator.

It was becoming clear that many of the prisoners were simply killed as soon as they arrived at Auschwitz. This is why the camp didn't need wooden huts for them all.

For Pilecki it was the start of more than two years of fear, pain and unimaginable misery. While he and his fellow prisoners slowly starved, they were forced to do hard, physical work, day after day. Their unwashed clothes became infested with foul-smelling lice – tiny biting creatures which carry diseases and cause skin irritation. The unsanitary conditions caused a terrible sickness called typhus to sweep through the camp, killing hundreds

of prisoners. The guards seemed to enjoy dishing out the most ferocious punishments, even when everyone followed all the rules. Other prisoners killed themselves by deliberately climbing onto the electrified fences.

Despite the extreme personal hardship, and his fear of being discovered, Pilecki worked hard to establish a resistance movement inside the camp. He soon had dozens of inmates stealing food and clothing. This was given to prisoners who had fallen ill, or to some who were kept hidden to prevent them being taken away and shot. The volunteers also did what they could to upset the guards' routine, although this did more to keep the prisoners' spirits up than to make their lives any safer or more comfortable.

At the same time, Pilecki arranged for information about life in the camp to be smuggled out to the Polish resistance. Most of all, he wanted the government in London to hear about it. By now gas was being used to kill more than a thousand Jews every day and their dead bodies were being burned to hide the evidence. Auschwitz, Pilecki said, needed to be bombed as soon as possible. He knew it would be much better to kill everyone inside (including himself) than to allow the camp to expand so that even more innocent civilians could be taken there and murdered.

Tragically, much of what he said simply wasn't believed. Many people thought it was too awful to be true. RAF officers hated the idea of bombing innocent prisoners, and anyway they didn't have any aircraft that could fly far enough into Poland to drop bombs on the giant camp.

After two and a half years in Auschwitz, Pilecki realised that no one was coming to help. With two other prisoners, he made a plan to escape through the camp bakery, taking with him stolen documents to prove what was going on. Amazingly, the plan worked and, although he was shot and slightly injured, he eventually managed to make his way to Warsaw, the Polish capital, nearly three hundred kilometres away.

Pilecki was only forty-two, but he now looked like an old man and years of harsh treatment in the camp had made him weak. Despite this, he rejoined the Polish resistance and took part in the Warsaw Uprising, the largest single revolt against the German army. The Poles had very few weapons and knew they stood almost no chance of success against thousands of German troops armed with aircraft, tanks, machine guns and heavy artillery. Despite this they showed many astonishing examples of courage, but in the end more than fifteen thousand members of the resistance were killed, nearly a third of them women.

Around the time of the uprising the British and Americans realised that Pilecki had been telling the truth all along, but they still refused to bomb Auschwitz. The killing was allowed to continue and by the time the war ended

an appalling six million men, women and children had been murdered by the Nazis, just because they were Jews.

Pilecki somehow survived both his years in the camp and the uprising, but when Poland was invaded yet again, this time by Russian troops, the new leaders had no interest in celebrating Polish heroes of the Holocaust. Witold Pilecki continued to campaign for his country's freedom until 1948, when he was arrested once more, this time by his own government. Falsely accused of spying against Poland, he was sentenced to death and then shot.

It was a terrible end for such a courageous man, but Witold Pilecki is now recognised around the world as a hero and a true humanitarian. He once said he had tried to live his life 'so that in the hour of my death I would rather feel joy, than fear,' and his selfless example is one that continues to inspire.

Pat O'Leary

A Doctor in Search of Adventure

Pat O'Leary was the code name of a Belgian army doctor who joined the British Royal Navy when his own country was invaded by Germany in 1940. Albert Guérisse decided not to tell anyone his real name or admit that he was a doctor because he wanted to do something more adventurous than treating the wounded. He went on to run a network of secret agents and volunteers in France who helped around six hundred mostly British and American servicemen evade capture and escape back to England.

O'Leary found himself in France almost by accident. He was helping to land two SOE agents on a deserted beach one stormy night when his boat capsized and sank. He swam hundreds of metres in the dark to reach dry land and was promptly arrested. Anyone suspected of being a spy risked being shot, but O'Leary tricked the police into thinking he was just an unlucky Canadian pilot. They believed his story about crashing his aeroplane into the sea and sent him to a prisoner-of-war camp full of British soldiers.

O'Leary **managed to escape** a few weeks later and fled to Marseilles, a large port city on the coast of the Mediterranean. There he joined forces with a young Scottish army officer who was trying to help others like him flee to Spain. When the Scotsman was arrested and locked up, O'Leary took over the dangerous job of organising his network of agents.

O'Leary needed to remain hidden to do this, but he also needed money. It cost a lot to smuggle someone out of the country under the noses of thousands of German guards. Many mountain guides were professional smugglers who wouldn't do anything without being paid. Some guards could be persuaded to pretend not to notice people slipping over the border into Spain, but only in return for money. And of course everyone involved needed shelter and food, which were very expensive without the right paperwork and official ration cards.

To pay for all this, O'Leary used his charm to convince a British cloth company to give him large sums of money in French francs. He promised the

company that the SOE in London would pay it back in British pounds. It was the perfect arrangement.

One of O'Leary's first jobs was to arrange for his Scottish friend to be smuggled out of the country. The officer had managed to escape from prison dressed in a stolen German uniform which O'Leary had arranged to be delivered to him. He was now hiding out with an old lady and a grumpy cat called Mifouf. Marie-Louise Dissart talked a lot, smoked non-stop and made Mifouf wear a little red jacket. The police dismissed her as an eccentric, but it was a clever disguise: Dissart was really a member of the Resistance. She helped O'Leary get his friend out of the country and went on to hide, disguise and feed an incredible 250 British and American servicemen before the war ended.

The escape network that the two ran together became known as the Pat Line. O'Leary was brilliant at identifying men and women he could trust. He began recruiting French agents as well as Scots, Australians, Greeks and even Germans, many of them Jewish, who wanted to help defeat Germany's ruling Nazi party and its leader, Adolf Hitler.

People started to arrive from all over France hoping O'Leary and these agents would get them to safety. Some were airmen who had crashed or been shot down. Others were French or Belgian soldiers who

wanted to get to London so they could rejoin what was left of the army and fight alongside the British. The agents called these people 'parcels' as a way of disguising what they were up to.

One of the Pat Line's **most important parcels** was an Englishman called Airey Neave. He was the first person to escape from Colditz Castle, a famous prisoner-of-war camp which the Germans believed was the most secure in Europe. Travelling by train and on foot, he managed to cross Germany without being recaptured. He then made his way through Switzerland before arriving in France. With the help of O'Leary he made it back to London and eventually went on to become a Member of Parliament.

Identifying genuine parcels was one of the hardest and most important jobs. O'Leary and his Pat Line colleagues worked hard to spot people attempting to join their organisation who were really spies or traitors. Usually they were good at this, mostly because O'Leary would only deal with people he personally trusted. Wherever possible checks would also be made with London to see if a person was really who he or she claimed to be.

But although O'Leary and his agents were cautious and careful, it only takes one small mistake to put an entire network in danger. When one of the Pat Line's wireless operators was captured by the Germans, O'Leary realised that he and his colleagues might not be able to continue operating for much

longer. The operator was a young Australian called Tom Groome. He had

made the mistake of transmitting a message without arranging for a look-out

to wait outside the building. This meant there was no one to warn him that the

Germans had detected his signal and were coming to arrest him.

The frightened Groome was taken away for interrogation, but then surprised

everyone by suddenly diving out of an open window onto the street ten metres

below. He was quite badly hurt by the fall, but managed to hobble away to

hide in a doorway further down the street. Unluckily, when the police rushed

out to look for him, a bystander pointed out Groome's hiding place and he

was taken back into captivity.

The arrest left the Pat Line agents without any way of communicating with

the SOE in London. When a group of five escaping airmen were arrested not

long afterwards, on their way to Spain, O'Leary became suspicious of one

of his recent recruits. He guessed that this new man might be working for the

Germans.

Despite the obvious danger, he arranged to meet the

man to ask him whether or not this was true. Unfortunately it was: O'Leary

was arrested on the spot and taken to Germany to be interrogated by the

Gestapo. For the next two years he was questioned again and again, and

frequently tortured. But whatever they did to him, he refused to give away any names or any details about his fellow agents. Finally, he was taken to the Dachau concentration camp and sentenced to be shot. Incredibly, the war ended before this sentence could be carried out, and O'Leary was released from prison and allowed to go home to Belgium.

Once there **he rejoined the army** and, as Albert Guérisse, he returned to his work as a military doctor. During an entire lifetime spent helping others in this way, he was awarded no fewer than thirty-seven different medals including the British George Cross.

Harry Cole

Double Agent: Working for the Enemy

For a spy operating undercover in a foreign country the greatest dangers often come from enemy agents rather than from the police or the army.

In the 1940s, several of Germany's top spies weren't German. In the same way that many of the agents sent overseas by the SOE in London weren't British, the German authorities employed men and women from other countries, including Britain. Usually these people swapped sides for money or because they thought Britain would lose the war and they wanted to be on the winning side.

Harry Cole was one of them. He was born in England and grew up in Hackney, which was then a poor part of London. As a young man he was jailed at least twice for fraud and for stealing money. When he was released from prison at the start of the Second World War, he lied about his criminal activities so that he could join the British army and fight in France.

For a while Cole seems to have been quite a good soldier and he was quickly promoted to the rank of sergeant. It didn't take long for him to start stealing again, and he was soon arrested and locked up when the army realised that some of its money had gone missing. When Germany invaded France, Cole became a prisoner of war, but he managed to escape. He stole a small car from a French family and drove hundreds of kilometres south to Marseilles, where he began working for the Resistance.

Once again, he didn't tell anyone that he was a thief or that he had been in prison. He told people that his name was Paul Cole and that before the war he had been a policeman at Scotland Yard in London. He also pretended he was a captain in the British army, a much higher rank than sergeant.

Cole told lies like this all the time, but he worked hard and members of the Resistance found him very useful. People liked him and when the SOE in London found out what he was doing they were impressed. They could see that Cole was courageous and quite clever,

and that he was doing a good job helping airmen escape back to Britain through Spain. But not everyone trusted him. Pat O'Leary, as one of the most important escape network organisers, was beginning to get suspicious about Cole. He was sure that the Englishman had stolen some of the money that had been sent from London to help the Resistance.

O'Leary asked a couple of his own agents to keep a close eye on Cole. It soon became clear to them that he was stealing money, and that he spent much of it eating in expensive restaurants and buying Champagne in nightclubs. Some Resistance members confronted Cole at an address in Marseilles and asked him if it was true.

Cole admitted straight away that he had stolen money, lots of it, but no one knew what to do with him so he was locked in the bathroom while they discussed it. Obviously he couldn't carry on working for the Resistance when no one trusted him, but he couldn't be allowed to go free either because he knew too many of their secrets. Eventually they decided he should be shot, but by this time Cole had climbed out of the small bathroom window and run away.

No one can be sure what happened next except that Cole now began working for the Germans. It's possible that the Gestapo caught him and forced him to do this, but he may just have switched sides in exchange for payment.

Whatever the reason, the Englishman started handing secret information over to the German police almost immediately. This included the names and addresses of spies who he knew were operating in France, and of members of the Resistance. He also provided maps showing the routes the agents used to get servicemen out of France, and more than thirty pages about the escape lines and how they worked.

The result was catastrophic for the British and French, and for the people they were trying to help. Many of the agents who were arrested were tortured and then killed, and it is now thought that Cole may have been responsible for as many as 150 deaths. This makes him one of the worst traitors in the whole of the Second World War.

For a while the authorities in London were still convinced that Cole was one of their agents and not a double agent working for the Germans. Cole continued stealing money so that he could carry on enjoying himself. He persuaded one girlfriend to give him all her life savings, and married another one after learning that she worked for an escape network. He tricked her into thinking he was a British agent, but she ran away when she found out the truth. Afterwards she always slept with a gun under her pillow in case Cole came looking for her.

Later, when it became obvious that Germany was going to lose the war,

Cole tried to switch sides yet again. This time he told the Americans he was a British agent called Captain Mason and that he could help them catch Germans. He nearly got away with it too, but then he came under suspicion after writing a note to a girlfriend bragging about what he was doing.

Before long he was being hunted by the British and French authorities who were determined to put him on trial. It didn't take long to catch him, but he managed to escape the first time he was arrested by disguising himself as an American soldier. However, the second time the police found him, hiding in a flat above a bar in Paris, they were better prepared. Cole was armed and managed to fire a few shots before the police responded with a hail of deadly bullets. The Londoner's luck had run out at last, and a few days later Harry Cole's bloodstained body was buried in an unmarked grave.

Claus Helberg

A Death Race on Skis

Norway was one of the first countries to be invaded by Germany at the start of the Second World War, but thousands of Norwegians were determined not to be beaten. In 1941 they formed their own resistance movement, known as Milorg.

Around the same time, Britain discovered that German scientists were trying to build a uniquely powerful new bomb. To do this they needed a chemical called 'heavy water' which was produced by a large factory located in a cold and remote mountainous region of Norway. The SOE in London began training a small team of four Norwegians who knew the area well. Their job would be to return to Norway and lead a group of British commandos to the factory to blow it up.

The four men were called Jens-Anton Poulsson, Arne Kjelstrup, Knut Haugland and Claus Helberg. Their mission was so important, and so secret, that each of them was issued with a deadly cyanide pill. They were expected to swallow these if they were captured so that they would die before they could be tortured and made to give away any details.

In complete secrecy, they were flown to Norway overnight in a British bomber. After parachuting down into the snow-covered countryside, they hiked several kilometres and established a base in the mountains. Their first task was to lay out a landing strip on a nearby frozen lake so the commandos could arrive in two massive gliders.

The gliders were being towed from Scotland behind a couple of Royal Air Force Halifax bombers. However, this part of the mission went badly wrong when one of the bombers crashed into a mountain, killing the seven-man crew. The glider it was towing crashed into the mountain moments later, injuring many of the seventeen men on board. Shortly afterwards the second glider came down much harder than planned. This caused even more injuries and the commotion alerted the Germans, who realised that something suspicious

was going on. They rushed to the scene to arrest all the survivors, who were then taken away and shot.

The four Norwegians weren't on the mountain so they escaped arrest. They still had their poison pills and now knew for sure that they would be killed if they were caught. They also knew it would be weeks, maybe even months, before another group of commandos could be trained and flown over from Britain.

Such a small team couldn't attack the factory on their own, especially now that the Germans knew it was a target. The four men realised their original plan was now useless and decided the best thing would be to stay far away from the factory and hope they could survive the bitter Norwegian winter out in the wilds.

For three months they were holed up in a tiny wooden hut far from any sign of civilisation. Most days were spent trying to find firewood and food while avoiding German patrols. Some days they only had moss to eat, but towards the end of December one of the men managed to shoot a reindeer. This meant they had meat on Christmas Day, and Haugland used his army dagger to cut out some pretty little wooden decorations.

After living like this for nearly twelve weeks, the four men were finally joined by another team of six Norwegian SOE agents. They had flown over from RAF

Tempsford in another British bomber and parachuted down to a landing spot a few kilometres from the hut. Together the ten men set off for the gigantic, seven-storey factory.

The Germans were confident the factory was reasonably safe from attack. It was situated halfway up a mountain, surrounded by minefields and floodlights, and armed guards were posted on a bridge leading to the main entrance. However, over the course of the winter, the men guarding the factory had become careless and lazy. This made things slightly easier for the Norwegians. After climbing down a steep ravine and wading through a freezing cold mountain river, Helberg and the other Norwegians managed to enter the factory without meeting a single guard.

Working as quickly and as quietly as they could, the men laid explosive charges in and around the most important parts of the factory. The bombs were positioned very precisely to make sure that when they exploded, the equipment in the factory would be blown to pieces. Special timed fuses were used to give the men a chance to escape and, by the time the first explosion occurred, they were already making their way back across the mountain.

Several more explosions followed, taking just seconds to rip apart the equipment used to make heavy water. When he inspected the enormous damage the following morning, the German military

commander admitted it was the most impressive act of sabotage he had ever seen. He was naturally furious about this and within hours more than three thousand German troops were frantically searching the countryside for the saboteurs.

Incredibly, none of the ten men was caught.
Several of them escaped on skis to the Swedish border, hundreds of kilometres away. Two more made their way to Oslo, the Norwegian capital, and rejoined their comrades in Milorg. Only Claus Helberg headed back to the isolated mountain hut. He planned to stay in the region for a while to assist Milorg members in the local area.

He was almost at the hut when he spotted some tracks in the snow and realised the Germans had discovered the hideout. Helberg quickly turned to flee, but he had been spotted. Six soldiers chased after him on skis as he raced for his life. He was a talented skier and managed to lose five of them eventually, but after two hours the sixth was still on his tail and skiing closer and closer. Eventually the soldier pulled out his gun and fired. Helberg fired back and the two men continued shooting until both had run out of ammunition.

The soldier, who may have been injured, suddenly gave up, turned around and went back. Helberg didn't stop to find out why. He was desperate to get as far away as possible and skied on as night began to fall around him. This was a big mistake as in the darkness he accidentally skied over a precipice. He broke his arm as he fell to the ground. The pain was agonising, but he dared not stop and forced himself to carry on.

After an incredible sixty-five kilometres

skiing with one arm, Helberg came to a house where he thought he would be safe. To his horror it was full of German soldiers! Helberg had to think quickly. He told them that he had been working as a mountain guide for a different group of Germans and said he had broken his arm while helping to look for the factory saboteurs. Incredibly, they believed him, and took him to see one of their doctors. Afterwards he checked into a local hotel.

But Helberg wasn't safe yet. Moments later, two senior German officers came into the hotel. Everyone in there was arrested and interrogated, and then eighteen of them were put on a bus to Grini, a prison camp in Oslo. Helberg was one of the eighteen. He knew that if the Germans found out he was a member of the resistance he would be shot like the British commandos, but he wasn't ready yet to take his deadly pill.

There was an armed guard on the bus, but Helberg was determined to escape. Things looked really desperate and he decided his best chance of avoiding capture would be to jump off the moving bus before it reached Oslo.

Helberg waited until it was dark and then, when the guard was distracted, he threw himself against the door. It burst open and Helberg hurled himself out onto the road. The bus was moving quite fast and unfortunately he landed on his broken arm. The pain was excruciating, but before he could even cry out, he was almost blown up by a grenade thrown out of the bus by the guard. Scrambling to his feet, Helberg ran as fast as he could into the forest by the side of the road. This gave him some cover and the guard realised it would be almost impossible to find him in the dark. After a few minutes the bus drove on, leaving the injured Helberg behind.

Relieved, but in terrible pain, Helberg eventually managed to reach a hospital where his injuries could be treated. After three weeks in a hospital bed he slowly made his way back to England. He returned to the mountains when the war ended, and became one of Norway's most famous ski guides as well as a national hero.

Scotch Lass

Britain's Smallest Secret Agent

It is hard to believe now, but on many wartime missions a pigeon was one of the most important pieces of equipment that a secret agent could take when parachuting into enemy territory.

During the Second World War, radio transmitters were huge, heavy and often unreliable. SOE agents couldn't risk using an ordinary telephone line because it might be bugged, but they still needed to communicate with headquarters. Pigeons like Scotch Lass provided an unlikely but effective way for them to do this, although it could be even more dangerous for the birds than for their human comrades.

The birds are called **`carrier or homing pigeons`**.  They were useful to the agents because they have an instinctive ability to find their way home. No one really knows how they do this or how they are able to navigate over huge distances. Pigeons have been known to fly more than 1,500 kilometres across mountains, featureless deserts and even oceans in order to reach home. Over shorter distances the birds have been recorded flying at speeds of around ninety-five kilometres per hour, which is amazingly fast when you think a pigeon weighs only a few hundred grams. Because pigeons can navigate even when starting from a place they have never visited before, hundreds of agents carried these birds on missions when they needed to send secret messages back to Britain.

Agents couldn't carry boxes and baskets, so the best way to carry a bird was often to put it into a woollen sock, which the agent could then hide in a jacket pocket or under one armpit. When the agent needed to send a message, he or she would write it down, often in code, on a narrow strip of paper. The paper was rolled up and put inside a tiny metal cylinder attached to one of the bird's legs. The bird would then be released and allowed to fly off. Hours or even days later, once the bird had reached its owner's home in England, the message was removed from the metal canister and taken as fast as possible to the SOE headquarters in London where it could be decoded.

During the Second World War, over the course of three years, agents took more than sixteen thousand birds into France, Belgium, the Netherlands and other countries occupied by the enemy. Sadly, only about a tenth of them made it back to England with their secret messages, which shows how dangerous the flights were for these astonishing birds.

The birds' instinct to fly home is such a strong one that we know they won't just have flown off somewhere else or decided to stay behind in the country where they had been taken. Some of those which didn't make it back to England probably died of exhaustion after flying into stormy weather over the North Sea or the English Channel. Others were killed by birds of prey (many of which eat pigeons) or shot down by enemy soldiers who recognised the threat they represented. Although the German authorities worked out what the British were doing with the birds, they sometimes showed a sense of humour about it. One bird arrived home late with a new message in its canister. This said, in German, 'We are returning your pigeon because we already have enough to eat.'

Scotch Lass was **one of the lucky ones** who made it home to England. She was trained in Suffolk at the start of the war and had successfully completed more than forty flights home from Royal Navy vessels in the North Sea before being selected for Special Duties. In the autumn of

1944 she was parachuted into the Netherlands with an SOE agent called Jacobus Groenewoud.

Groenewoud had become an agent after being told he wasn't fit enough to join the army. After training with the SOE he secretly travelled across the North Sea to collect information about the enemy forces which had occupied the Netherlands four years earlier. By this time Dutch citizens were under pressure to collaborate with the German invaders. Many did, but Groenewoud was determined not to. He wanted to help the resistance movement.

The British and American governments were desperate to find out about troop movements in occupied Europe. They needed details about how many soldiers there were, and about the weapons they used and the buildings they had taken over. Groenewoud's mission was to gather this information and then send it back with Scotch Lass in the form of dozens of tiny microphotographs.

Microphotography was an ingenious way

of sending a huge amount of information in the smallest possible space. The information could include photographs (for example of a railway depot or power station that the RAF was planning to bomb) or several pages of documents. Each photograph had to be re-photographed and then dramatically reduced in size. Written or typed documents were treated in the same way so that more than a dozen lines of text could be contained in a

single mark like a full stop, known as a microdot. The words could only be read using powerful magnifying equipment.

These microphotographs were so small that Groenewoud was able to fit nearly forty of them into the tiny canister attached to one of Scotch Lass's legs. Each contained a mass of useful information and, although the actual secrets have never been revealed, we know that back in London the SOE was desperate to see them.

Unfortunately, when Groenewoud released Scotch Lass it was early dawn and in the half light she crashed into some overhead electrical cables almost immediately. She fell to the ground and began flapping her wings awkwardly. Seeing that she was injured, Groenewoud rushed forward to pick her up. He was worried about the bird, but most of all he wanted to retrieve her canister so that the precious microphotographs could be sent with another pigeon.

However, before he could grab Scotch Lass, she seemed to recover slightly. She rose clumsily into the cold early morning air and, by the time Groenewoud reached the spot where she had fallen, the resilient bird was circling high above him, preparing for the long journey home.

Despite Scotch Lass's injuries she somehow managed to cover more than four hundred kilometres back to England. This took her over the sea, which pigeons hate, and across countryside she had never seen before. The journey took many hours, but miraculously she made it back to her home loft in Suffolk. The canister was quickly removed and the microphotographs were raced down to London on the back of a motorbike to be analysed by the SOE.

For an injured bird it was **an incredible achievement**, but Britain's smallest secret agent was too badly hurt to go on any more missions. Instead, at the end of the war, Scotch Lass was awarded the Dickin Medal, this country's rarest and most important award for animals in wartime.

Josephine Baker

No One Suspects a Star

Everyone knows about the fictional spy James Bond, but in real life the most successful agents are the secretive and anonymous ones. Their lives can be adventurous, but they are rarely glamorous: spies need to stay hidden to survive. They need to look like ordinary people and make it look as though they lead ordinary lives.

There are a few exceptions to this, however, and one of the most extraordinary was a woman called Josephine Baker. Baker left school aged eleven or twelve, and for a while she was homeless, before discovering that she could dance. She got a couple of jobs performing on stage in New York, but in the 1920s life was hard for black entertainers working in the US. Baker decided to travel to Europe and was convinced she would have an easier life in Paris, the French capital.

It turned out she was right. Baker very quickly **became a star** and after a tour of Europe she returned to Paris to appear at its most famous theatre, the Folies Bergère. Every night, hundreds of Parisians queued to see her dancing. She usually wore very exotic costumes (one of her skirts was made out of pretend bananas) and sometimes she appeared on stage accompanied by a pet cheetah called Chiquita and Ethel the chimpanzee. Chiquita's collar was studded with real diamonds.

Baker starred in several films and sang in an opera, and by the 1930s she had become the best-known American living in France and one of the country's richest stars. She even went back to the US to star in a big Broadway musical, but Baker's old friends could all see that she now preferred Paris to New York and that she wanted to go home.

By now the glamorous American loved Paris more than anywhere on earth. In 1937 she married a Frenchman and a couple of years later, at the start of the Second World War, she agreed to work as a spy for the French

military. Her fame gave her the freedom to travel around the country giving concerts. Everywhere she went fans flocked to see her. These included many VIPs, such as foreign military officers and high-ranking embassy officials, who were delighted to meet the lively and beautiful celebrity at parties after each performance.

As well as German officials, Baker met diplomats from Italy and Japan. Both of these countries were fighting on the German side, so Baker encouraged the people she met to gossip. She carefully memorised anything they said which she thought might be useful to the French authorities or to her friends in the Resistance.

When Germany invaded France she carried on travelling, although now it was only possible to visit neutral countries like Spain and Portugal, which were not taking part in the war. All the time Baker stayed alert to news about the fighting. She eavesdropped and continued collecting any information she thought might be valuable. As well as passing on military gossip to members of the Resistance, she recorded the names of airfields and harbours which were being used by the German navy and air force. She also memorised details of how many troops the Germans were moving around France.

Some of **this information was secretly sent** to London. She wrote down names and numbers in invisible ink on pages of sheet music. As a performer, she could carry these from country to country without suspicion. At other times she pinned notes and even photographs inside her underwear, assuming (and hoping) that no one would dare to stop and search such a famous woman. Fortunately she was right. Most of the border guards just wanted her autograph, and Josephine Baker was never searched.

In 1941 one of these journeys **took her out of Europe** and across the Mediterranean into North Africa. The explanation given to the public was that the star was suffering from pneumonia and that she hoped the warm African sun would do her good. In reality Baker was going to Africa to help the French Resistance, and to make contact with members of a British spy network. This brought her into yet another secret organisation, one which supplied Jews with Moroccan passports so they could escape from the Nazis by fleeing to South America.

Finally, after appearing to recover from her illness, Baker put on a number of special concerts in North Africa to entertain troops from Britain, France and the US. Civilians weren't allowed to attend, but any serviceman who came along was given a free ticket. This did a lot to raise troop morale, helping to keep their spirits high at a time when the war with Germany wasn't going very well. It also made Baker even more wildly popular than before.

Baker took many personal risks to do all this, but the enemy never caught up with her and she survived the war. She was made a Chevalier of the Légion d'Honneur by the French president, and awarded the Croix de Guerre medal, two of France's highest awards. In peacetime she continued to put her fame and popularity to good use. In the US she refused to perform in segregated clubs and theatres (where black and white audience members were not allowed to sit together) and she became known as a passionate supporter of human rights.

Later, celebrating nearly fifty years in showbusiness, France's most famous and most surprising spy gave a concert in London in front of Her Majesty the Queen. Today she is remembered around the world for fighting racism and for her enduring belief in the idea that people of all nationalities can live together peacefully.

Andrée Borrel

Dropped into Danger

Most SOE agents in the Second World War were sent abroad under cover of darkness, usually by boat, submarine or aircraft. Spies were also dropped by parachute, but in the early 1940s only men were taught how to do this. The army had thousands of male paratroopers, but it took several years for anyone to think of training any of the SOE's female volunteers.

The first to take the plunge were Andrée Borrel and Lise de Baissac, both of whom had managed to escape from France after the German invasion in 1940. Borrel had worked as a fashion designer and then an army nurse before she joined the Resistance. Once in England, she was approached by the SOE.

She was only twenty-two years old, but the SOE knew about the dozens of stranded Royal Air Force pilots she had helped before she left France. Lise de Baissac was thirty-seven and was employed as a journalist. She spoke excellent English as well as French and had been asked to join the SOE after they recruited her brother.

In September 1942 the two women found themselves somewhere over the English Channel, sitting cross-legged on the metal floor of a cold, cramped Armstrong Whitworth Whitley bomber. This was their second attempt to return to France. On the first occasion their aircraft turned back because the pilot had been suspicious about the lights laid out on the ground by the Resistance to show him where to drop the agents. He was worried that the two women were parachuting into a trap and he refused to let them jump.

They made a second attempt the following night. Neither of the women said much to each other during the flight. They were too nervous to talk and anyway the bomber's powerful Rolls-Royce engines made too much noise for them to hear anything else. Eventually a member of the crew appeared and removed a panel in the aircraft's floor, leaving a gaping black hole. It was time to jump. Borrel went first and de Baissac followed a couple of seconds afterwards. They had drawn straws before take-off to decide who would jump first.

Both of them landed in a meadow outside a town called Mer, where they split up. Borrel had orders to make her way to Paris, about a hundred kilometres away. De Baissac went to Poitiers, a smaller city situated further south, and her story is told in the next chapter.

Borrel had been born and brought up in Paris so she knew it well. Her mission involved joining the Prosper circuit, the same group of Resistance volunteers as Noor Inayat Khan had joined. Prosper was involved in weapons training and sabotage. It also supervised weapons drops in which supplies of submachine guns, explosives and ammunition were secretly parachuted into France by the RAF.

These supplies needed to be delivered to different Resistance groups in utmost secrecy and then quickly hidden from the Germans. It was dangerous work, but the members of the circuit were very impressed by Borrel's performance. She was tough, but easy to like, and her energy, her calmness under pressure and her enthusiasm for the job were clear to see. In only a few months the young woman was promoted. She was now the circuit's second-in-command and led several attacks against enemy installations, including one on an important power station.

Her success was impressive for such a young agent, but then one night in June 1943 Borrel was suddenly arrested. Along with several other circuit members, she was taken to 84 Avenue Foch, a building with a fearsome reputation. This was the Gestapo's main interrogation centre for this part of France. Prisoners were regularly brought from the nearby Fresnes Prison and locked in tiny cells on the top floor.

It's still not clear how the enemy found out about Andrée Borrel and her comrades. On the floor below, several captured British wireless sets were being used to send fake coded messages which sounded as though they came from the SOE in London. It may have been one of these that tricked someone in Borrel's circuit into giving away their location, or perhaps the Gestapo had its own spy in the Resistance. However it happened, she now found herself in enemy hands.

Not much is known about her interrogation except that Andrée Borrel displayed a complete contempt for her captors. If she was scared she didn't show it and she refused to answer any of their questions. Eventually the Germans realised they were wasting their time trying to get any information out of her. She was returned to Fresnes Prison after each interrogation and then, after months of this, handcuffed and forced onto a train bound for Germany.

At this time Germany operated a sinister scheme called *Nacht und Nebel* (meaning 'night and fog'). Spies working for the British or for the Resistance were simply made to disappear if they couldn't be persuaded to swap sides. Because Borrel had refused from the start to say or do anything useful to her captors, the Germans regarded her as a highly dangerous individual. In 1944 she was taken to a prison camp with three other female SOE agents, including Sonia Olschanezky, who had blown up a German train full of ammunition. Shortly afterwards, all four were brutally murdered using lethal injections.

Andrée Borrel was still only twenty-four years old but had lived an extraordinary life. She had always shown huge determination to succeed and was completely committed to the dangerous life she had chosen for herself. After her death the French and British governments both recognised her sacrifice by awarding the Croix de Guerre and the King's Commendation for Brave Conduct in her name.

Lise de Baissac

Living Next Door to the Enemy

Many SOE agents were sent into Nazi-occupied countries during the Second World War with orders to help existing groups of partisans in their fight against the enemy. Lise de Baissac was different: she was given the task of establishing an entirely new group of freedom fighters in the French city of Poitiers.

Her training for this had been extensive. Before leaving England she was taught, like dozens of other agents, how to fire different kinds of guns and how to pick locks. She learned how to crack open a safe or blow one up, and how to burn down a building or set light to a train. De Baissac was even given survival lessons by one of the gamekeepers employed on the King's country estate at

Sandringham in Norfolk. He showed her how to catch, kill and skin a rabbit in order to avoid going hungry, although de Baissac wasn't convinced that she would ever need to do this.

If she was bored by all the training she didn't show it. At the end de Baissac's report said that she was one of the very best students and that she had shown she could be 'cool and collected in any situation'. An agent in enemy territory certainly needed those qualities, and as if to prove how cool she was, de Baissac moved into an apartment next door to the Gestapo's own headquarters.

She called herself Madame Irene Brisse. If anyone asked she told them she was a widow and that she had moved down from Paris because living in the capital was too expensive. Her plan was to run the apartment as a safe haven where other agents could come for help, equipment and information. Being close to the railway station made it convenient for this, but having the Gestapo building so near meant that using a wireless transmitter to call London was much too dangerous.

To begin with she was extremely lonely.

She didn't know anyone in Poitiers and it was hard finding anyone locally who would help her. Simply asking people if they were in the Resistance (or whether they wanted to join) would have been far too risky. Building a network of useful contacts was a slow and difficult job.

One of de Baissac's most important tasks involved cycling far out into the countryside looking for remote places where agents could safely land by parachute and where the RAF could drop supplies of weapons and explosives. She had to travel even further whenever she needed to send or receive a message. It was more than three hundred kilometres to Paris, where she could use a radio transmitter. She could visit her brother Claude in Bordeaux – he was also an SOE agent and his job was to keep an eye on German ships and submarines. Unfortunately Bordeaux wasn't much closer than Paris.

De Baissac worked hard and made good progress, but it still took several months before the new circuit was up and running. By this time she was in regular contact with three other Resistance groups, but it wasn't long before the Gestapo became suspicious of all three. De Baissac and Claude had to escape back to England, which was frustrating for them both.

De Baissac **was determined to return to France** as quickly as possible, but this was hindered when she broke her ankle while teaching two new recruits how to parachute. It took months for her to be declared medically fit and it wasn't until 1944 that the SOE decided she was well enough to go back to France to help her brother deliver weapons to the Maquis.

The Maquis were armed gangs of French men and women who hid out in secret locations, often high up in the mountains. Like the Resistance, they risked their lives doing whatever they could to make things difficult for the enemy. Assisted by agents like Lise and Claude de Baissac, members of the Maquis became skilled at sabotaging railway tracks by blowing them up and attacking German trains carrying soldiers towards the coast. This was vitally important work, especially in 1944 when Britain and its allies were planning the D-Day invasion of France.

While the Maquisards were busy planting explosives, slashing the tyres of military vehicles and cutting communications wires, de Baissac spent her time cycling up to sixty kilometres a day and sleeping in ditches each night. She needed to travel considerable distances to deliver arms and explosives to various different Resistance groups, with instructions about where they should strike next.

She also **took part in several armed attacks** against the enemy and had two very lucky escapes during her many close encounters with German police and soldiers. On the first occasion, she was stopped and searched by German troops, but fortunately they didn't find the radio components or the code books she had hidden under her clothes. The second time she was even luckier. Returning to a house that she had been staying in, she walked into her bedroom to find it full of soldiers. One of them

was sitting on her bed, actually on her British parachute, but he didn't seem to realise what it was. None of the soldiers spotted the packets of English sweets in the kitchen either, which would have given the game away. Calmly, and as cool as ever, de Baissac walked out of the house and made her escape once again.

After the liberation of France, Lise de Baissac went back to England. For a few years she worked for the BBC as a newsreader but then returned to southern France, where she married an artist. The rest of her life proved to be much quieter than the early years, and Lise de Baissac was nearly a hundred when she died in 2004.

Margery Booth

Singing for Hitler

Margery Booth was a rare thing in Adolf Hitler's life: somebody English whom he liked and thought he could trust.

Booth was born in Wigan in Lancashire and trained in London to become an opera singer. Beginning as a teenager, she won numerous prizes for her performances and went on to perform at the Royal Opera House. After travelling to Hollywood to make a movie, she married a German and moved to Germany.

In 1933 Booth was chosen to appear on stage at the world's most famous opera festival, in the German town of Bayreuth. This was the same year that Hitler became Germany's new leader and he was in the audience one night. He was transfixed by the elegant young woman and her beautiful voice, and when the curtain came down he rushed round to her dressing room to congratulate her on her performance.

The following morning Booth received a giant bouquet of red roses. These were wrapped in a Nazi banner covered in swastikas, and the card accompanying the flowers simply said 'Adolf'. On a later occasion the two of them had dinner together.

By 1939 Booth was performing with the prestigious Berlin State Opera, but once Britain and Germany went to war she was classified as an 'enemy alien', someone from a hostile country. Ordinarily this would have meant being sent to a prison camp (despite being married to a German), but Booth avoided this, almost certainly because Hitler was such a big fan.

Her singing was popular across Germany, but Booth never forgot she was British. She had already begun to take advantage of her special position before the war, by passing details back to British Intelligence of the conversations she had with important German military and political officials. Once the fighting started, she was determined to do even more. Her chance came when she was given permission to entertain

British soldiers at a prisoner-of-war camp outside Berlin called Stalag III-D.

The prisoners loved it when she stepped onto the stage to loudly announce 'I'm Margery Booth from Wigan,' before singing a selection of well-known English songs. After one performance Booth discovered that a prisoner in the audience was a spy, and despite the risks, the two of them agreed to work together.

The spy inside Stalag III-D was John Brown, a British army sergeant who had managed to persuade the Germans that he was really on their side. He told them he could recruit other prisoners who would join the German army if they were released. In fact, what he really wanted to do was to identify potential traitors and collaborators inside the camp so that he could report them to MI6.

The Germans appeared to trust and like Brown, which made him extremely unpopular with many of the other prisoners, but by pretending to be a traitor he was able to smuggle information out of the camp in letters using code, which the guards failed to spot. When he met the English opera singer, he realised she could provide him with another way to send secret information back home.

Booth was keen to help him do this, and on at least one occasion she gave a concert with several pages of confidential notes hidden in her knickers. Unfortunately, because the double life she was living had to remain secret, stories reached England of the singer's friendship with Adolf Hitler. This ruined her reputation in Lancashire. At one point her family disowned her, and many of her British fans were deceived into thinking that she wanted Hitler to win the war.

This could not have been further from the truth, and in Germany people were slowly becoming suspicious of both Brown and Booth. Eventually the pair were arrested by the Gestapo and accused of spying. Brown managed to escape, and although Booth was tortured she bravely refused to say anything that might incriminate either of them. She was finally released because the Germans couldn't prove anything. She fled from Berlin during a bombing raid, then slowly made her way back to England.

After the war, the evidence the pair had supplied to MI6 was used to prosecute several of the most notorious traitors, including a famous one with the nickname Lord Haw-Haw. For his part in this, Sergeant Brown was recognised as a hero and awarded the Distinguished Conduct Medal. However, Margery Booth received nothing and, because people still thought she had been Hitler's friend, her career as a singer never recovered. She attempted to start a new life in the United States but died of cancer before

she could enjoy anything like her pre-war success. After she had worked so hard and even risked her life as an agent, Margery Booth's death seems even sadder because her heroism and patriotism were never really acknowledged in her lifetime.

Alix d'Unienville

Miss Moneybags

Alix d'Unienville was born in Mauritius, an island in the Indian Ocean. Mauritius had once belonged to France before becoming a part of the British Empire, so many of the islanders spoke both French and English really well.

As well as being multilingual, d'Unienville had the ability to blend into a crowd. People who knew her said she was the type of calm, quiet person whom no one would ever suspect of being a spy.

D'Unienville very nearly didn't become a secret agent though. When she was first approached, in 1943, the twenty-five-year-old was so surprised that she forgot to write down the address of the place in London where she was meant to go for an interview. She stopped a taxi and asked the driver if he knew of any top secret buildings in the area which were full of foreigners like her. He laughed at the idea and repeated her question to several other taxi drivers. They also thought it was funny, but eventually someone suggested the Special Operations Executive HQ at 64 Baker Street.

She went along and passed the interview easily, but still had to train before being parachuted into France. D'Unienville travelled to a secret camp in Hampshire, the mysteriously named House in the Woods, where she and several other agents were taught all sorts of specialist skills over the next few months. These included how to make duplicate keys and force locks, different ways to break into properties or to survive for long periods out in the wild, and even how to silently poison an aggressive guard dog.

These trainee agents also learned how to fire weapons and jump out of an aeroplane, although d'Unienville's instructors were worried that such a slim young woman wouldn't be strong enough to control her parachute in a fierce wind. She was determined to show them that she could do it, although it took several successful practice jumps before they agreed

that she was ready to be sent on a mission.

The SOE instructed d'Unienville to go to France to act as a courier for various Resistance group fighters. This was lonely work and highly dangerous because anyone travelling around the country during the German occupation was likely to be stopped by the police. If that person was also caught with a large amount of money or anything which looked like a coded message, he or she was certain to be arrested and interrogated.

Although **carrying a lot of money** made a courier's job dangerous, in d'Unienville's case it also saved her life. When she finally parachuted into France, she was carrying a fortune in French banknotes. Most of these were packed into a heavy travel bag, but about two million French francs were strapped to her back. Agents were warned at the House in the Woods that any parachute jump could go wrong, especially in the dark. D'Unienville's did just that when the material of her parachute got caught up in the branches of a tall tree as she came down. When she freed herself and dropped to the ground, the thick wad of notes on her back protected her by breaking her fall.

Once safely down, d'Unienville hurried to the capital. She spent the next three months distributing vital funds to different Resistance groups in and around Paris, and carrying secret messages from her flat above a fruit and vegetable shop. If anyone asked, she said her name was Aline and that she was married. Her husband, she said, was a prisoner of war.

At the end of the three months she arranged to meet another SOE member on a street corner outside one of Paris's big department stores. Unfortunately they were spotted by a pair of German agents before they could exchange any information and make their getaway. Both were arrested, bundled into a black car and then driven to the dreaded Gestapo headquarters on the Avenue Foch.

When the Gestapo searched d'Unienville, they found the cyanide capsule often issued to SOE agents, which naturally made them more suspicious. They also found a railway ticket in her pocket, but d'Unienville managed to swallow this before they spotted the address of one of her contacts written on the other side.

However, after questioning the cool young woman, the Gestapo still couldn't be absolutely sure she was a spy. They weren't sure what to do with her, so she was taken from Avenue Foch to a nearby prison while they thought about it. Now d'Unienville wasn't sure what to do either. She decided to pretend to be mentally ill. With a bit of luck, she thought, the Germans might think she was wasting their time and let her go.

The ruse didn't work and very soon d'Unienville found herself on a train heading for Germany. This must have been a lot more frightening than being in a prison cell in Paris. D'Unienville may not have known that several SOE agents had been murdered in Germany, but she would certainly have realised that the further she travelled from France the harder it would be for her to escape.

By an amazing stroke of luck, the Allies (the countries who joined forces to fight the Nazis were called 'the Allies'), chose this moment to bomb the railway line and a bridge over the River Marne was badly damaged. The train couldn't go any further, so the guards ordered all the prisoners to get out of the carriages and walk across the bridge to the next village.

Halfway across, d'Unienville considered jumping off and plunging down into the river, but it was very high and she didn't rate her chance of survival. Instead she took advantage of the disruption and when the group reached the village she ducked into a house while the guards were busy trying to restore order. The owners, an old French couple, were horrified at first and for a moment d'Unienville thought they might give her away. Luckily the opposite happened. The old man silently gestured for her to go upstairs, where she hid until the other prisoners had been led away.

This lucky escape turned out to be the final chapter in her career as a secret agent. D'Unienville's face had become too well known for her to carry on working undercover, so for the next few months she remained in hiding until the Germans' final retreat and surrender. After the war Alix d'Unienville took to the air once again, but this time without a parachute. She joined the French national airline as one of its first female crew members, and later became a bestselling author.

BANQUE DE

Jeannie Rousseau

Wrecking Rockets

It wasn't only the Resistance groups that used the talents of spies to fight back against the Nazi occupation of France. A few French men and women began secretly spying against the Germans on their own.

One of these was twenty-one-year-old Jeannie Rousseau. She had been an outstanding student at university in Paris before moving to the town of Dinard with her family. She was particularly good at languages, including German, and after the invasion of France she realised she could put her talents to good use by getting a job as an official translator. This work brought her into regular contact with German army officers and she began to hear interesting things from them about wartime steel and rubber production.

These were both essential raw materials for manufacturing military trucks and tanks, and it didn't take long before Rousseau had a lot of useful information about the enemy's plans. To begin with, she didn't know what to do with the information. 'I was storing my nuts,' she later said, 'but I had no way to pass them on.'

She was always very careful about what she asked the officers and didn't tell even her parents what she was doing. After a while, though, the German commanders began to get a bit suspicious of this quiet, intelligent young woman and her questions. She was arrested, but she didn't admit to anything and was eventually released, although she was ordered to move away from the area. This was because Dinard was on the north coast of France, exactly where the Germans were planning to launch their invasion of Britain.

Rousseau was not put off by this. She went straight to Paris and got another job working for a group of businessmen whose companies supplied raw materials to the German army. Once again, she found she was in a perfect position to gather secret information, but again she had no one to pass it on to.

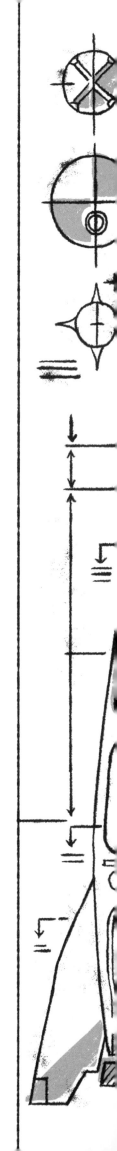

This all changed a few weeks later when she met a man on a crowded late-night train. He recognised her from university and they stood together as there were no free seats. They got chatting and, after a while, he suggested they should work together. The man told her he was a member of the Resistance and that he belonged to a small group of agents called the Druids. If Rousseau joined them, any secret information she obtained could be passed to the Resistance and sent on to the British secret service.

Rousseau agreed to do this. She went back to work the next day even more determined to listen out for any information which could be useful to the Druids. It was much too dangerous to write any of it down, but she had what people call a photographic memory. This meant she could remember a lot of what she saw and heard in incredible detail.

Because she was charming and spoke their language so well, many of the German officers Rousseau met really enjoyed talking to her. She had a trick of pretending that she wasn't very clever and that she didn't really understand what they were talking about. This encouraged the officers, rather foolishly, to describe their work in greater detail, even though much of it was classified as top secret.

During one of these conversations Rousseau heard something about two new weapons that Germany was building to attack Britain. These were called the V-1, a kind of jet-powered flying bomb, and the even larger V-2 rocket, which could fly at more than 5,500 kph. Neither of them needed a pilot and they were incredibly hard to shoot down because they were so fast. Both types could fly more than 150 kilometres before exploding, which made it possible to hit London and many other cities never previously within reach.

The weapons sounded so terrible to Rousseau

that she resolved to find out as much about them as she could. She listened carefully as several foolish officers, determined to impress her with how advanced German weapons were, began to share important military secrets.

One officer actually let her look at some drawings of one of the rockets. More than anything, he wanted her to see that Germany's weapons were superior to the ones the British had. This time Rousseau really couldn't understand the information. She wasn't an engineer, and the drawings were very, very complicated, but thanks to her photographic memory she was later able to pass on some astonishing details to her friends in the Resistance.

A report on the weapons was sent to London. British intelligence chiefs couldn't believe how good Rousseau's information was. V-1s and V-2s had already begun to devastate parts of several English towns and cities, and eventually killed more than six thousand men, women and children. The report contained precise details about where the weapons were being built

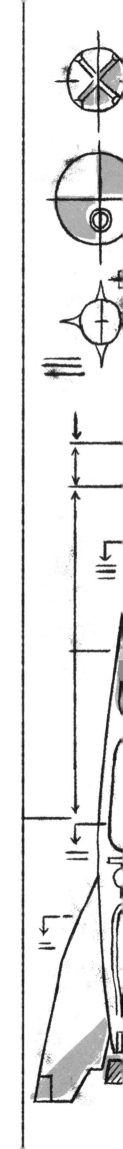

and where the launch sites were hidden. Mostly these were spread out along the coasts of Belgium and northern France.

The information supplied by Rousseau and other agents meant that the British and American air forces could send hundreds of bombers across the North Sea to attack the factory and destroy the launch sites. Disrupting Germany's weapons programme in this way turned out to be crucial in reducing the number of deaths caused by V-1s and V-2s. However, it did nothing to make Rousseau's position in France any safer and she was arrested for a second time while trying to escape to England.

This time the Gestapo **weren't taking any chances** and the translator they had never quite trusted was sent to prison. Over the next few months, she was moved in and out of various German concentration camps. Each new place seemed worse to her than the last one. At one, Ravensbrück, the guards were particularly brutal. Vicious beatings happened every day, and more and more prisoners died of disease or were murdered. For those prisoners who survived, food rations were reduced to starvation levels.

Towards the end of the war Rousseau caught tuberculosis, a lung disease, and became extremely sick. She was convinced she was dying and after a while the guards began to believe this too. Eventually she was rescued and nursed by members of the Red Cross, and incredibly she made a full recovery.

Despite the dangers and **terrible hardships** of her early life, Jeannie Rousseau lived to be ninety-eight. Like many of her generation she preferred not to speak a lot about the war and for many years she refused to accept medals from the French government and the US Central Intelligence Agency (CIA). She was an old lady before she agreed to tell her story to a journalist, but by the time she died she was acknowledged as a national hero.

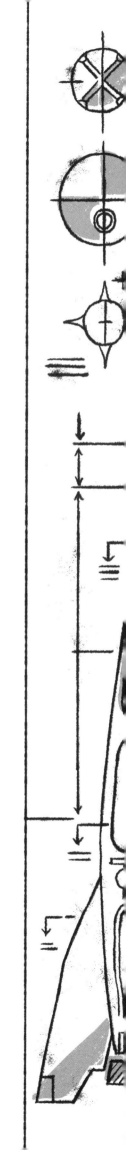

Harry Rée

Teacher Turned Factory Saboteur

Harry Rée, a school teacher from the north of England, became a conscientious objector at the start of the Second World War. This meant he refused to fight because he thought it was wrong to kill another human being. Instead of going into the army he joined the National Fire Service and began rescuing people who had become trapped in burning buildings during air raids.

After two years, however, Rée changed his mind because he was horrified by Germany's treatment of the Jews. One of Rée's grandparents was Jewish, so Rée volunteered for the army before joining the Special Operations Executive. His main task at the SOE was assessing men and women who wanted to be

agents. His work involved finding out if they had the right skills and the right

personality to be sent overseas. The more of them that Rée met, the more

fascinated he became by the dangerous life of a secret agent. Eventually he

decided to train as a radio operator and asked to be parachuted into France.

At first his request was turned down because he knew too much about how

the SOE worked. A senior officer at the London headquarters was worried he

might give them away if he was ever caught and interrogated or tortured. Rée

refused to give up, and when the officer left to do a new job he applied again

and this time was given permission.

His mission went wrong almost immediately.

When he jumped out of the aeroplane he was accompanied by a large

metal canister containing weapons and radio equipment. This had its own

parachute, which got tangled up on an electricity pylon. Rée couldn't climb

the pylon to pull it down, and it was too far from the ground for him to reach,

so all the equipment inside it had to be abandoned. Rée realised that the

canister would be spotted as soon as the sun came up and the enemy would

know that an agent had landed somewhere nearby.

He got away as quickly as he could, but when he arrived at the hotel where

he was supposed to be staying under a false identity, Rée discovered that

it had been taken over by the Gestapo. It was full of Germans so he had to

keep moving. Fortunately, he managed to contact another agent a few days later, only to be told his northern accent was so strong that no one would ever believe he was French!

The agent told Rée to go back to England, but Rée was determined to continue his work and decided to hide out in the Jura mountains instead, on the border between France and Switzerland. There he joined forces with some of the Maquis resistance fighters. When he was a conscientious objector Rée had hated the idea of bombing towns and cities because this killed thousands of innocent civilians. Watching the Maquis, he became convinced that the best way to defeat the German army was sabotage, by destroying the equipment and machinery its soldiers needed to carry on fighting.

Rée turned out to be brilliant at this. After months of training and hard work with the Maquis, he came up with an idea called blackmail sabotage. This involved persuading French collaborators (people who were co-operating with the Germans) to turn against them and help the Maquis instead. Sometimes the best way to do this was with threats.

Rée's first really big target was the giant Peugeot car factory at Sochaux. During the war, car manufacturers stopped building automobiles and began making military vehicles instead. In the US, for example, the Ford Motor Company built nearly ninety thousand bomber aircraft, and the workers at

one factory were so efficient they completed a new bomber every fifty-five minutes. These were coming out of the factory so fast that pilots were allowed to sleep there so they could take off as soon as their aircraft were ready.

The factory at Sochaux employed more than sixty thousand people, making it easily one of the largest in Europe. When Germany invaded France the Peugeot family were allowed to keep their factory, but they were ordered to stop making cars and make only tanks and aircraft for the German army and air force.

Some workers at the factory were extremely unhappy about this. They didn't want to help the Germans and even before Rée arrived on the scene several had begun risking their lives to disrupt production. The easiest way for a person to achieve this was to do his or her job really badly. Before long around half of the vehicles leaving the factory had something wrong with them.

In 1943 `the factory was bombed by the RAF`, but the raid went badly wrong. The factory buildings were hardly damaged, but 125 people were killed and more than 250 injured when most of the bombs fell on hundreds of French homes. Rée watched the air raid from his hideout and was appalled by the deaths and widespread destruction. He also realised that the people risking their lives to build faulty vehicles couldn't do this fast enough to make a real difference to the war.

He decided to make a secret telephone call to Rodolphe Peugeot, the family member who was in charge of the factory. He told Peugeot that he could persuade the RAF to stop bombing it, but only if the family promised to help the saboteurs working inside their company. Rée said this would stop hundreds, maybe even thousands of workers being killed in another air raid and it might save the family business.

Rodolphe Peugeot was highly suspicious

at first because he didn't know who he was speaking to. Rée understood this and so arranged for a message to be sent from London. The message was enough for Peugeot to change his mind and several members of the family became secret but firm supporters of the Resistance. The first thing Peugeot did was to arrange for Rée to visit the factory (in disguise) so that he could plan a really effective attack. After this, instead of bombing the factory, the RAF began dropping supplies of explosives which were carefully hidden inside it.

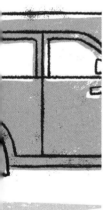

Rée told his agents to place the explosives around the most important pieces of machinery inside the factory. Once this was done, they waited until all the workers had gone home and then lit the fuses. At midnight there was an enormous explosion and then another. Several heavy steel doors were blown nearly twenty-five metres into the air and a gigantic machine called a press was almost completely destroyed.

The factory itself survived, but it was out of action for several months so no more vehicles could be produced. The press had been used for making tank turrets and when the Germans organised a new one to be delivered by barge, another sudden explosion sent it to the bottom of the canal.

The Gestapo began questioning members of the Peugeot family, but couldn't prove that any of them had arranged for their own machinery to be blown up. Rée, however, quickly came under suspicion. He was tracked down by a policeman and shot four times. One bullet punctured his lung and another grazed his heart, but incredibly he escaped by hitting the policeman over the head with a brandy bottle and biting off his nose.

Despite his injuries, Rée managed to swim across a river and then crawl painfully for several kilometres to reach Switzerland. He was helped over the border by a courageous teenager called André Graillot, and managed to make it back to England before the war ended. In peacetime he returned to teaching, but said nothing about his activities in France. By the time he retired, the modest war hero had become a highly respected university professor.

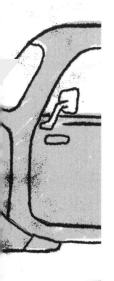

Mary Lindell

The Incredible Escape Artist

Mary Lindell married a French aristocrat and lived in Paris, but she was very rude about his country and many of its people. She thought that France had surrendered much too quickly when the Germans invaded in 1940. She was determined to do something about this and convinced her children to help free the country from enemy occupation.

Lindell's marriage to the Comte de Milleville made her a countess, but although she had a grand French title, and gave all three of her children French names, she was most proud of being English. She refused to carry a French passport and when the police became suspicious about her British one, she just shrugged and lied about it. She told them that she had always hated England and everyone who lived there.

Life in France under the Nazis was extremely dangerous for anyone English, even for a person as tough and strong-minded as Lindell. She had been awarded several medals during the First World War for her work as a battlefield nurse and now felt it was her duty to stay in France and fight. She wrongly believed that the French wouldn't stand up to the Germans and thought that people like her needed to show them what to do.

Lindell's real skill was helping people in danger to get out of the country. She set up her own escape routes through occupied France and began rescuing refugees as well as stranded British soldiers, secret agents and airmen. According to her daughter, this hazardous work became an obsession and soon it was the only thing Lindell was interested in doing.

Many people found her difficult to deal with as most of the time she was bossy and rude. She hated anyone getting in her way and once hit a fellow nurse. Her voice was as loud as a foghorn, but she was extremely good at what she did. She was also incredibly brave and refused to be scared off when a French traitor deliberately crashed a car into her, knocking her unconscious and breaking several of her ribs.

In 1942 Lindell and her family successfully smuggled out the only two survivors of a daring British raid. Twelve Royal Marine commandos with canoes had been dropped close to the French coast by submarine. Their plan was to paddle for several kilometres towards a group of German ships under the cover of dark, then attach magnetic bombs called limpet mines to the ships' hulls and slip away unseen. Six vessels were damaged when these mines exploded, but tragically ten of the commandos were never seen again. Most of them were caught by the Germans and killed, and two died when their canoes capsized in the rough sea.

The British authorities had no real idea about what had gone wrong until Lindell sent a message saying she had rescued the last two men. One of her sons and his girlfriend had taken them from France into Spain using one of Lindell's secret escape routes across the Pyrenees mountains. 'The whole area', she said, 'was swarming with Gestapo, traitors and troops, but they got through safely.'

Later, both her sons were arrested. Octave was taken to Germany, where he died in mysterious circumstances. His elder brother Maurice was locked up by 'the Butcher' Klaus Barbie, the notorious Gestapo leader who liked to torture his prisoners.

When Lindell heard this, she sent her daughter, Barbé, to plead for his freedom. Barbé pretended to befriend several German officers and asked one of them how much it would cost to get Maurice released. He explained that this was not legally possible, but admitted that if she was prepared to pay a bribe of more than thirty thousand francs something might be done.

This was a lot of money, but fortunately Lindell had enough. She carefully tore all the banknotes in half and made two piles. She handed one pile over to the Gestapo. They could have the other pile, she said, only when her son had been released. Amazingly, this was successful, which must have surprised her. However, the Gestapo were now aware of her and knew that she had something to do with the Resistance.

This didn't seem to worry Lindell much, if at all. She just changed her name to Marie-Claire and disguised herself using her old nurse's uniform. Although this had several British medal ribbons sewn on to it, Lindell was able to carry on with her rescue efforts. She and her children managed to help around a hundred people from Australia, Britain, Canada, Greece, New Zealand and South Africa to escape before anyone saw through her disguise. This time she was arrested and put on a train with armed guards.

Lindell had been locked up at least once before, after loudly insulting some German officers. This time it looked a lot more serious, and she decided to

make a break for it. Taking a huge risk, she jumped off the moving train, but one of the guards saw what she was doing and shot her in the head. Astonishingly, this didn't kill her and she was taken to a military hospital for a life-saving operation. After being nursed back to health, she was put on another train bound for Ravensbrück, a women's concentration camp in Germany.

Lindell didn't try to escape from the camp, but she decided to make a nuisance of herself by being as awkward as possible. She constantly taunted the guards by telling them how Germany was losing the war and that anyone who mistreated a prisoner would be severely punished when it was all over. She also refused to follow orders, even when the guards threatened to shoot her again, and told them she was only prepared to work there as a nurse. Eventually they agreed to this, which made it possible for her to look after the sick and injured prisoners and to get them a little extra food.

When the Red Cross inspected the camp, the Germans insisted they didn't have any British or American prisoners behind bars. Lindell quickly proved that this wasn't true. She had secretly compiled a list of all their names and as a result more than twenty women were released from the camp. The evidence collected by Lindell also ensured that after the war a total of thirty-eight guards and other officials, many of them women, were charged with war crimes committed inside the camp. Most were found guilty.

Mary Lindell returned to France and despite all her rude comments about the French, it remained her home until she died aged ninety-one.

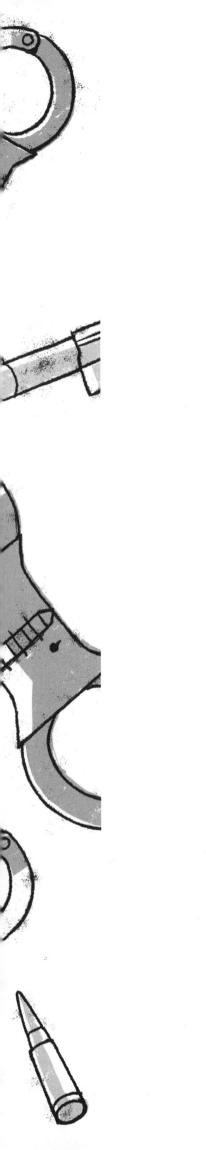

Krystyna Skarbek

The Powers of Persuasion

When the author Ian Fleming sat down to write his first ever James Bond adventure he may have used a real-life spy as the inspiration for one of the characters in *Casino Royale*. Fleming's most glamorous agent has a lot in common with Krystyna Skarbek, a Polish member of the Secret Intelligence Service (MI6). She was the first female agent to be sent into occupied Europe, and spent more time abroad than any other woman working for the British secret service.

Skarbek was popular and had a reputation for being completely fearless. Her MI6 file described her as 'a flaming Polish patriot, an expert skier and a great adventuress' – all things which came in useful during her first mission.

When the German army invaded Poland in 1939, Skarbek was sent from London to Hungary, where she managed to persuade an Olympic skier to guide her across the snow-covered Tatra mountains. Winter temperatures in the mountains plunged as low as -30°C, but this looked like the best way to sneak unseen into enemy territory. Unfortunately, almost as soon as she arrived in Warsaw, the Polish capital, she was recognised by an old friend. The two had known each other for years, but Skarbek was a brilliant liar. She was able to convince her friend that she was someone entirely different and that the two of them had never met before.

After this nerve-racking encounter, Skarbek began travelling around the country on foot, by train and even on horseback. Her job was to organise a network of Polish spies to keep a close eye on enemy troops. They did this by watching the road, rail and river routes to and from Germany. They also smuggled information out to MI6 in London and captured a new kind of anti-tank gun which they hoped British manufacturers could copy for use against the enemy.

Skarbek hid the gun at an apartment in Budapest in Hungary. Hungary wasn't at war yet, but the local police were suspicious of anyone travelling in and out of Poland. Before long, the German Gestapo began keeping an eye on Skarbek.

Shortly afterwards, **she was arrested and questioned** for several hours. By this time, she had been spying for more than a year, but she insisted she was just a journalist and refused to say anything about her other activities. However, as the questioning got harder and harder, she thought they were going to torture her so she bit her tongue as hard as she could and began coughing up blood. This horrified her interrogators, who thought she had tuberculosis, a deadly infection spread by coughing and sneezing.

The Gestapo couldn't get Skarbek out of the building fast enough, but they decided to keep a close watch on where she went. She was smart enough not to do anything suspicious or to contact any other agents until she had given them the slip. Once she had managed to do this, MI6 arranged for her to get a new British passport (in which she was called 'Christine Granville') and she was driven out of the country hidden in the boot of an old car.

Skarbek knew she couldn't go back to Poland because the Gestapo would be looking for her. Instead she went to Egypt, where she contacted some members of the SOE. Although she gave them a precious roll of microfilm

(showing Germany was about to invade Russia) the organisation decided that she could only have an office job from then on.

Skarbek's problem may have been that her escape sounded too good to be true. Some of her colleagues thought she had made it up and that she was now spying for the other side. All she knew was that an office job would be much too dull for her. She decided to retrain as a wireless operator instead, and then to get onto a Royal Air Force parachute course. She already spoke French fluently and, once she had acquired these new skills, the SOE finally agreed to send her into France, where agents were badly needed.

One thing Skarbek wasn't very good at was firing a gun. Although some of the SOE's very best shots were women agents, Skarbek hated loud noises and always closed her eyes before pulling the trigger. Because of this, she probably didn't mind too much when she made her parachute jump into France and landed on top of her pistol. Luckily it didn't go off, but the gun was broken and she was left with a large bruise.

After making contact with members of the French Resistance, Skarbek set off for the mountains again. This time she headed for an isolated fortress in the Alps where a group of Polish prisoners had agreed to fight for the Germans in return for their freedom. After a two-day hike, Skarbek found the

men nearly two thousand metres up the mountainside. She was exhausted after the long climb but still managed to persuade more than two hundred of them to surrender their weapons. They abandoned the fort and joined the French Resistance.

Barely a week later she discovered that three of her comrades had been arrested and imprisoned. The SOE's forgery department had made a small mistake while faking their identity papers, and now it looked like all three would be shot as spies. Skarbek immediately went to the prison and began arguing with the senior Gestapo officer there, saying they should be released. The officer wasn't impressed, but Skarbek said she was married to one of the men and that she was related to General Montgomery, one of Britain's top army officers. None of this was true, but she was extremely convincing.

Next she told the officer that British troops were on their way to surround the prison. When they arrived, she said fiercely, he would be severely punished, maybe even shot, if her comrades had been mistreated in any way. This wasn't true either, but she was a brilliant liar and after listening to her for nearly three hours the Gestapo officer finally gave in. The three men knew nothing about any of this and still expected to be executed as they were marched through the prison gates. Instead they found a car parked outside, waiting to drive them away.

Krystyna Skarbek's audacious lies, and her refusal to back down, had saved their lives, but unfortunately her own life did not have a happy ending. After the war the French and British governments awarded her several medals to recognise her courage and service, but she was then murdered by an ex-boyfriend on a visit to London.

Didi and Jacqueline Nearne

The Spies Who Were Sisters

Two young sisters who escaped from France to England in 1940 were determined to do something useful after their brother joined the Royal Air Force.

Jacqueline and Eileen (nicknamed Didi) found they could only get boring jobs. Their father was English, but many people in London were suspicious of anyone arriving from a country which was occupied by the Germans.

When the sisters applied to join the Special Operations Executive they hit another obstacle. Both were described as unintelligent by one of the people who interviewed them. Another said Didi was scatterbrained and not very practical, and that neither woman could be recommended for anything top secret.

Luckily a more senior officer took a completely different view. The two young women both spoke excellent English and French, and he felt certain they would be able to blend in perfectly once they were in France. In his opinion, Jacqueline was one of the most impressive applicants that the SOE had ever seen, and Didi was a highly convincing liar. Like all the best spies, he thought, she was a great actor.

Jacqueline was authorised to parachute

into northern France as soon as she had completed her training, but not so Didi. She was still only twenty-one and before leaving for France her over-protective big sister had got the SOE to promise not to send her overseas. Because of this, Didi had to stay behind in England, where she was employed as a signals operator. Handling secret messages from agents overseas could certainly be interesting (sometimes they were written in invisible ink on the back of supposedly ordinary letters) but she still longed to do something more exciting like her sister's job in France.

Jacqueline was now in a small group helping to organise a succession of sabotage missions against the enemy. These included blowing up an aircraft engine factory, destroying major railway lines, setting fire to dozens of army trucks and stealing more than twenty tonnes of precious fuel. At times she found herself in charge of hundreds of Resistance fighters, but it was exhausting and dangerous work. There had already been several attempts to arrest her and, after surviving undercover for more than a year, Jacqueline was ordered to return to England for her own safety.

She was unhappy about this, but she knew **she had no choice**. Worse still, when she got back to London, Jacqueline discovered that Didi was no longer there. She had pestered the head of the SOE's French section for so long that eventually he had given in and agreed to send her to France. As it turned out, her skills at this sort of persuasion would later prove extremely useful.

Jacqueline found out that Didi was still working in signals, but now she was the person sending the secret messages rather than the one receiving them. It wasn't what she wanted to hear. These messages were vital if the Resistance was to get the money and weapons it needed from Britain, but working as a wireless operator was extremely dangerous. In fact, Didi was almost caught the very first time she travelled across Paris with her heavy equipment.

A German soldier on the same train had demanded to know what was in her suitcase. Didi pretended to be a shop assistant and told him it was a record player. She said she was going to visit friends to play some music and then got off at the next stop, before the soldier could demand to look inside the suitcase. Didi decided to make the rest of that journey on foot, but every time she needed to send a message to London she ran a similar risk of being discovered by the special radio detector vans that were roaming around Paris.

Over the next five months, Didi sent more than a hundred messages without being caught, but it was becoming harder and harder each time. It helped that she kept moving from place to place, but Didi knew her luck would run out eventually.

Her final message was transmitted from a secret address on the edge of Paris to the SOE back in London. As soon as she had finished tapping out the Morse code, Didi heard a commotion in the street outside. When she looked out of the window, careful not to be spotted, she could see armed men running down the road towards the building.

Knowing she had less than a minute before they were at her front door demanding to be let in, Didi sprang into action. She stripped the wireless equipment down to its components and quickly hid the parts around the room. She found somewhere else to hide her pistol, and

then stuffed all of her coded notes into the oven. She could only hope they would have time to burn completely before anyone made it into the house.

Luckily they did, but once the Germans started their search it didn't take long to find the hidden radio components. Didi was arrested and taken away. Because no one had found her gun or the codes, she pretended she didn't know what was going on. When she was accused of being a spy, she just looked surprised and denied it. When the Germans told her they knew she had been sending messages, she said she had been doing it for her boss, a businessman, and had no idea what the messages were about. She stuck to this story and, although it all sounded a bit unlikely, Didi's performance must have been convincing. Before long, her interrogators were completely confused. Was she an agent, they wondered, or was she just a stupid young woman caught up in something she didn't understand?

Desperate for an answer, they tried hitting her and torturing her, but she refused to tell them anything more. Even when they tried almost drowning her in a cold bath, Didi stuck to her story. Three times her face was held under the water, and three times she came out choking, gasping for air and still playing the part of the confused young woman who didn't know why she had been arrested.

Finally, her interrogators gave up. They couldn't be sure she was a spy, but they couldn't be sure she wasn't one either.

Her skill at deceiving them almost certainly saved her life, but Didi was sent to the first of a series of prison camps. Over the next few months, she was regularly beaten severely, but she still refused to change her story. Then, while being marched overnight to a new camp, she took advantage of the darkness and bravely made a run for it with two other female prisoners. The three hid out for several days in the forest, without food, and then in an old church tower where Didi collapsed from illness and exhaustion. Eventually they were rescued by American soldiers and Didi was returned to her sister in England.

Jacqueline and Didi **lived quietly together** after the war. When Jacqueline died aged sixty-six, Didi retired to Devon, but she said nothing to any of her neighbours about their extraordinary lives. The truth only emerged a few days after her own death, when a clutch of French and British medals was discovered in the eighty-nine-year-old's flat.

Charles Fraser-Smith

Gadgets and Gizmos

When British agents were sent overseas in the Second World War, they mostly had to rely on their wits and their courage, but occasionally organisations provided something extra – and very often this came from the fertile imagination of Charles Fraser-Smith.

Fraser-Smith's school report had described him as 'useless except for woodwork and science and making things', but his common sense and practical approach to problem-solving came in handy when he spent several years living and working in North Africa.

After moving back to England, Fraser-Smith was asked to give a talk about his time abroad. In it he mentioned something called 'bricolage', the name given to the process of making use of whatever you can find lying around. Two government officials in the audience were so impressed by his ingenuity and inventiveness that they invited Fraser-Smith to London. After a short interview he was offered what he later described as a funny new job.

Officially this involved something boring to do with government clothing supply. Unofficially Fraser-Smith was given the task of producing secret gadgets and gizmos which agents and members of the military could use when they were operating behind enemy lines.

For someone with Fraser-Smith's love of innovation it was a wonderful opportunity and, together with a department known as Section XV, he spent the next few years devising a series of extraordinary things. Most of these were intended for members of MI6 and the SOE, but other items were designed to help the thousands of prisoners of war who escaped and needed to find their way back to Britain.

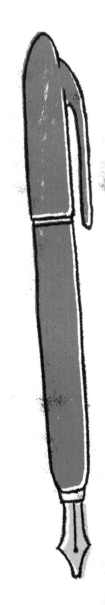

Some of his ideas were simple but ingenious, such as a hollowed-out shaving brush that could be used to hide rolls of

microfilm or secret codes. This had a base which could only be unscrewed by turning it the 'wrong' way. Fraser-Smith had a theory that anyone trying to open it by turning the handle of the brush anti-clockwise would give up before realising it unscrewed in a clockwise direction.

He was right, and soon the same idea was being used on a variety of other secret containers. These included hollowed-out fountain pens, golf balls, wine bottle corks and fake cigarettes. Fraser-Smith became an expert at hiding anything from a compass to a tiny telescope in items which looked like something else. Section XV went on to design a cigarette lighter which concealed a tiny working camera, a miniature radio the size of a cigarette packet, and even fake camel poo which would explode and blow the wheels off any military vehicle that drove over it.

Other inventions were rather more gruesome. Fraser-Smith painstakingly stitched steel giglis into pairs of bootlaces. A gigli was a flexible saw made of sharp wire. It could be used to silently strangle an enemy combatant, or to cut through bone if an agent needed to amputate a finger or two. Fraser-Smith was also asked to produce a very special canister large enough to contain a dead body. (See the next chapter for more on this.)

Section XV even sought to play a role in sabotage by creating one of the most bizarre pieces of equipment of the entire war.

This was an exploding rat, which was made by hollowing out the carcass of a genuine dead rodent. The cavity was then filled with plastic explosive and the skin stitched back over.

The idea was that an agent could hide a couple of these rats in a railway station coal stack. When the coal was shovelled into the furnace of a steam locomotive, the whole train would be blown off the rails. Unfortunately, the Germans found out about the plan before it could be put into operation properly. They found the grisly idea so fascinating that pictures of the booby-trapped rats were shown to students at military academies in Germany to warn troops to be vigilant.

Secret maps and compasses sound a lot less spectacular, but they were badly needed because, until the war, most Britons had never been abroad. A working compass could be made from a magnetised razorblade or paper clip (or made small enough to fit into a button on an airman's uniform) but one of Fraser-Smith's most imaginative devices was a smoker's pipe which contained a compass and a tiny map, yet could be smoked just like any other pipe.

Larger maps were printed on silk scarves and handkerchiefs using a special type of ink which only became visible when the agent urinated on it! Silk was expensive, but it was much better than paper because it was very thin and could be folded into a tiny square. Silk could also survive being submerged

in water if an aircraft came down in a lake or the sea. Other fabric maps were stitched into clothing to prevent them being discovered if an agent was arrested and searched.

Although Fraser-Smith could design clever gadgets like these, he often had to rely on outside companies to produce them. These companies were never told what the items were for. The man who supplied the rats, for example, believed they were needed for experiments in the animal laboratories at the University of London.

The world's oldest toymaker, Jaques of London, was the most famous company which manufactured items for Fraser-Smith and Section XV. The company was first contacted by an officer from MI9, the secret department for what spies called 'Escape and Evasion': helping prisoners of war and stranded pilots get back to Britain.

By law, prisoners of war were allowed to write to their families and to receive letters and parcels from them. They would often ask for board games because life in camp was so boring. MI9 asked Jaques of London to manufacture a series of toys and games to be sent to these prisoners, of a sort never seen before. They looked completely ordinary, but contained highly detailed maps and forged documents hidden between the layers of cardboard used to make each game and its box.

Foreign banknotes were similarly hidden

in the special tools used for lacing up the prisoners' footballs, while other games contained concealed compasses and tiny hacksaw blades. One of the company's most famous products, the Staunton chess set, was specially produced with hollow chess pieces containing different coloured dyes. These could be used to alter a soldier's uniform to make it look more like civilian clothing – but only if the user remembered to open the piece by unscrewing it the wrong way . . .

The name Charles Fraser-Smith is not well known today, although his cunning and ingenuity helped save the lives of numerous agents and escapees. His clever gadgets have not been entirely forgotten, however, and many 007 fans believe he was the original inspiration for the character of Q, James Bond's ever-inventive colleague.

'Major Martin'

The Man Who Never Was

One of the most unusual tasks given to Charles Fraser-Smith in his work with

Section XV was to design a metal canister large enough to contain a human

body. He wasn't told whose body, but it was an important part of one of the

most secret, most audacious missions of the entire Second World War.

In 1943 Britain and its allies were planning to invade Europe to free

France, Belgium and other countries from years of enemy occupation. The

invasion was going to begin with an attack on Sicily in southern Italy, but it

was important to keep this secret. The Allies believed that if the Germans

could be tricked into thinking that the invasion was going to take place

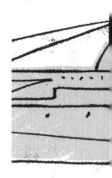

somewhere else, their troops would face less opposition when they landed.

A plan was devised to make the enemy think the invasion was really going to begin hundreds of kilometres away on the beaches of Greece and the island of Sardinia. It was codenamed 'Operation Mincemeat' and involved placing a dead body in the sea off the coast of Spain with a briefcase padlocked to its wrist. This would contain information about military plans which looked top secret but was really fake. Spain was chosen because although it wasn't involved in the war its government was very friendly with Germany. If the Spanish police thought Sardinia and Greece were about to be invaded, they would almost certainly warn their counterparts in Germany.

The dead body had to be genuine, and it had to look as though it belonged to a British officer who had drowned after his aircraft had crashed into the sea. It would need to be dressed in the right kind of uniform, and the uniform would need to have convincing evidence in its pockets that the wearer was a real person who had died in a tragic accident.

Obtaining a corpse was extremely difficult. No one could know about Operation Mincemeat except the team planning it. This made it impossible to approach an undertaker, or even an ordinary family who had suffered a loss. At the same time, the authorities were not prepared to allow a body to be stolen and used without the family's permission.

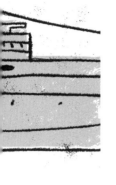

The problem was solved when the body of an unemployed, homeless Welshman was found near a railway station in central London. Investigations revealed that Glyndwr Michael hadn't been married and that his parents were both dead. Without a family there was no need to seek permission, so the top secret plan could now be put into operation.

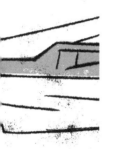

The first thing was to transform Michael's corpse into that of an imaginary officer in the Royal Marines called 'Major William Martin'. The correct uniform was duly obtained, but one of the hardest things to find was the right kind of woollen underpants because clothing was rationed and in short supply.

'Major Martin' was also supplied with a set of `false identity` documents. To make things look even more realistic, a photograph of an imaginary girlfriend called Pam was tucked into his wallet along with two love letters and a receipt for a diamond ring. A pair of ticket stubs from a West End theatre were also provided, along with a letter from his bank and a bill from the Naval and Military Club.

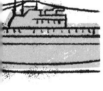

All this was to make it look as though the major had enjoyed a brief stay in London before setting out on his mission. The plotters hoped this would help convince the Spanish that Martin was a real person, but the most important document was a faked letter tucked into the locked briefcase. This appeared to be from one senior British general to another and discussed the forthcoming

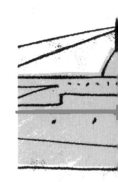

invasion of Greece and Sardinia. MI5 scientists conducted tests on various different inks to make sure that the writing would still be visible after being immersed in seawater.

All this took time to arrange, so the corpse had to be kept at a low temperature to preserve it. When it left London, Fraser-Smith's ingenious canister would ensure that the body didn't decompose before it was slipped into the sea off the coast of Spain. He did this by packing a chemical called dry ice around the body. As this dissolved, it would fill the canister with carbon dioxide gas, driving out any oxygen which would otherwise make the body decay.

When everything was ready, a racing driver called Jock Horsfall was employed by MI5 to drive the canister up to Scotland in a special van. He almost crashed at least twice because he was driving so fast, but several hours later the body was loaded on board HMS *Seraph*, a Royal Navy submarine bound for Spain.

The submarine's crew had no idea what they were transporting, but the captain had his orders. Once the *Seraph* neared the Spanish coast, he waited until dark and then took the body from the canister and released it into the sea. The team behind the audacious scheme had done everything they possibly could. Now, for the deception to work, they needed a lot of luck.

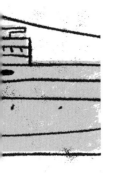

Some fishermen spotted the body early the following morning and pulled it out of the water. They reported their find to the Spanish police in the nearby port of Huelva. The police agreed to bury the body as soon as possible, because waterlogged corpses decay very quickly. However, before doing anything else, they carefully collected together all the different documents and the contents of Major Martin's pockets.

Because Spain was a neutral country it offered to return everything to Britain, although this was only done after Major Martin's paperwork had been closely studied and photographed. At the same time, somebody tipped off Germany's senior agent in Spain about what had been found drifting in the sea – and, unsurprisingly, he was desperate to see copies of the photographs.

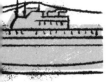

The British plan was working perfectly!

As soon as Karl-Erich Kühlenthal had his own copies, he raced back to Germany and the 'evidence' was presented to Adolf Hitler. It is impossible to know exactly what Hitler thought about Martin, his briefcase and the supposedly top secret letter, but shortly afterwards he gave the order to move ninety thousand soldiers from Sicily to Greece. At the same time, the number of German troops in Sardinia was doubled, and aircraft and torpedo boat crews were told to expect an invasion.

The Allied attack was launched a few weeks later. By the time Germany realised its mistake, realised perhaps that it had been tricked, it was far too late to move the troops back to Sicily and the invasion was successful.

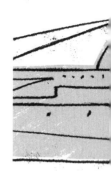

It took more than fifty years for the role played by a tragic, homeless man to be acknowledged, but in 1998 a gravestone in Huelva was modified to read GLYNDWR MICHAEL; SERVED AS MAJOR WILLIAM MARTIN.

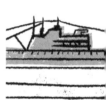

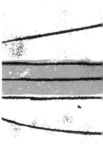

William Colepaugh

More High Life than Spy Life

When an American citizen announced that he wanted to join the German army, Berlin's intelligence chiefs devised a secret plan to send him back as a spy to help them understand more about some of the US's most advanced military technology.

Germany's secret service had tried sending spies to the US once before, but the mission had gone wrong almost immediately and all eight agents had been arrested. Now they thought an American might have a better chance of succeeding, although they weren't sure they could trust him. William Colepaugh had already been thrown out of the US Navy and he had a criminal record. Also he didn't speak a word of German and insisted he be paid tens of thousands of dollars in advance.

Because of this, it was decided to send an experienced German agent to keep an eye on him and in September 1944, Colepaugh and Erich Gimpel left Europe in a U-boat submarine bound for the US. The pair were ordered to investigate military shipyards, aeroplane factories and rocket-testing facilities. They were to send back their findings using a special short-wave radio transmitter which they would have to build for themselves in New York.

Gimpel had been trained as a wireless operator and he was given a set of plans showing how to build a working radio set. For security reasons these had been reduced to the size of a microdot so special equipment would be needed to read them.

German sailors knew there weren't many places in the US where it was possible for a submarine to approach the coast even at night-time without being seen. After lying on the seabed for more than a week to avoid detection, the U-boat captain decided to drop the two men at a remote beach near Bangor in the state of Maine.

Travelling by submarine is very slow, and Colepaugh and Gimpel were exhausted by the two-month voyage. Desperate to leave the cramped conditions and to breathe fresh air at last, neither of them picked up the machine needed to read the instructions for building the radio. It's possible they thought it was too heavy to carry up the rocky beach, or it may have just been forgotten.

As the submarine slipped back beneath the surface of the Atlantic, the two men began walking into town in the hope they would find a taxi to take them to a railway station. Unsurprisingly, they were spotted almost immediately and at least two people thought they looked suspicious walking along a country road in smart city suits. Also, neither of them was wearing a hat, which was unusual in Maine on a freezing November night. Luck was with the pair, however; they managed to find a taxi and, even more luckily, no one who saw them bothered reporting it until they were safely on their way to New York.

Once in the city, the pair rented an apartment where they hid their false identity papers, a couple of small pistols and a camera fitted with a special lens for photographing documents. They also had the money which Colepaugh had demanded (equivalent to more than £500,000 in modern currency) and nearly a hundred diamonds which they could sell in an emergency.

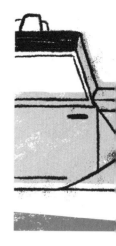

It was decided that Colepaugh should do all the talking because Gimpel spoke English with a strong German accent. Gimpel started the job of building the radio transmitter, which was almost impossible because he had no way of reading the instructions. He tried using a magnifying glass (which didn't work) and then decided to buy an ordinary radio which he could convert into a transmitter if he was able to get the right parts for it.

Buying the components was a problem, however. Gimpel couldn't risk talking in public because he sounded so German, and Colepaugh suddenly seemed more interested in enjoying himself than doing any work.

When Gimpel asked for help with the shopping, Colepaugh picked up a pile of money and went out to lunch. Later, when Gimpel said they should start recording the names and types of ships coming in and out of New York harbour, Colepaugh took another pile of cash and went off to a nightclub. Soon he had stopped coming back to the apartment and began booking rooms at some of the city's luxury hotels. He spent even more money on expensive meals and exotic cocktails.

Gimpel didn't like what he was seeing

and suggested they split up and go their separate ways. It's possible that

he thought he could carry out the mission on his own, but before he had a chance Colepaugh took nearly all of the money from the apartment and then disappeared with both guns and the special camera.

What had been planned as a two-year mission looked like it was already over in under a month. Even if the two men had done any spying in that time, which is highly doubtful, they had failed to send a single message back to Germany.

Worse still, Colepaugh was beginning to panic. Clearly it hadn't really occurred to him before what would happen if he was caught, but now he was worried. He knew the money couldn't last forever, and that if he was convicted of spying there was a good chance he would be executed like the previous eight had been. So he decided to give himself up and hoped that if he told the authorities all about the mission, and betrayed his comrade Gimpel to the police, they would let him go back to being an ordinary American citizen.

Barely four weeks after arriving in Maine, both men were under arrest. During interrogation, Colepaugh told the FBI everything in an attempt to avoid the death penalty. Gimpel said almost nothing as he was convinced he would be executed anyway.

Both were sentenced to death by a military court, but then told they would be given life imprisonment instead. Gimpel was released after ten years, and Colepaugh after fifteen. Colepaugh stayed in the US and seems to have changed his ways to become a law-abiding citizen. Gimpel went back to Germany and later wrote a book about the pair's extraordinary, but brief and unsuccessful careers as spies.

Elyesa Bazna

A Traitor Tricked

Elyesa Bazna was born in Albania but served in the French military until he was jailed for three years for stealing cars and weapons. When he was released from prison he found work as a doorman and a taxi driver before being hired as a domestic servant at the British Embassy in Ankara, the Turkish capital.

Turkey remained neutral for most of the Second World War, but each side in the conflict tried to persuade the country's leader, Ismet İnönü, to declare war on the other one. These attempts were mostly unsuccessful, although Turkey finally joined Britain and the US when it became obvious that Germany and Japan were going to be defeated. As a crossing point between Europe and

Asia, Turkey was a hotbed of undercover activities and many spies were active there in the 1940s.

Elyesa Bazna was one of these spies, although no one at the British Embassy realised it. Although his job was not an important one, he could read at least four languages and quickly realised that many of the documents passing through the embassy were ones which the Germans would find interesting. When he found out that Germany was prepared to pay him well for information he agreed to begin spying on its behalf.

Bazna was given the code name 'Cicero' and he began photographing the documents, secretly passing these to German agents. He found it quite easy because one of his jobs was guarding the study belonging to the British ambassador, the most senior official at the embassy. This gave him the opportunity to make copies of the keys he found in the ambassador's desk, including the one to the safe where the most secret and important documents were kept.

Whenever the ambassador took an afternoon nap or went to have a bath, Bazna locked the study door and opened the safe. Inside it he found documents describing details of Britain's military strategy, its troop movements around Europe and even the secret negotiations it was having with Turkey

about entering the war. These were all things which the Germans wanted to know more about, and Bazna handed over several rolls of photographic film in exchange for envelopes stuffed full of banknotes.

This went on for several months until eventually officials in London became suspicious. From listening in to German radio messages they knew they had a problem somewhere in Turkey, that somebody close to the ambassador was leaking British secrets to the enemy. Bazna was questioned, but it was decided that he was probably too stupid to be the brilliant spy the British thought they were looking for. An attempt was also made to trick the spy by planting a fake document in the ambassador's safe, but Bazna didn't fall for it so he kept his job.

Luckily for the British, some of the information he had been selling was so extraordinary that the Germans didn't believe that all of it could be true. When Bazna tipped them off about a top secret meeting in Iran between the Russian leader Joseph Stalin, US President Franklin D. Roosevelt and British Prime Minister Winston Churchill, they considered murdering all three of them. But when another stolen document revealed that Britain and the US were planning an attack on German forces in northern France, it was ignored in Berlin because the spy was supplying copies of so many documents that no one could believe they were all genuine.

British suspicions about the leaks made spying on the ambassador much harder, however. When an alarm was fitted to the embassy safe, Bazna suddenly announced that he was leaving to get another job. Even then no one realised that he was the embassy spy and Bazna was only caught after the war when he tried to buy a hotel using the money the Germans had paid him.

It turned out that most of the banknotes were fake and so Bazna was jailed again. This time it wasn't for treachery or theft, but for attempting to defraud someone by using forgeries, although until his arrest he probably didn't realise he had been tricked in this way. Bazna later took the German government to court in a shameless attempt to get the money he thought he was owed, but this failed and he spent his final years working as a nightwatchman.

Klaus Fuchs

Stealing Scientific Secrets

In 1940, two University of Birmingham scientists demonstrated that it would be possible to create a new type of weapon so powerful that a single bomb dropped from an aeroplane could destroy an entire city. Britain and its allies immediately began trying to build one, which they called a nuclear or atomic bomb.

Complex mathematical calculations made by Otto Frisch and Rudolf Peierls proved that a bomb containing only a few kilograms of a rare metal called uranium could cause more damage than thousands of ordinary bombs. Because uranium is radioactive, its explosive power is so much greater than a normal bomb that a single explosion could wreck thousands of buildings and kill even those people hiding in basements and cellars.

Although the devastation and death would be terrible, the British, American and Canadian governments recognised that a powerful bomb like this would enable them to win the war, but only if they could build one before Germany managed to do the same.

They created a vast organisation codenamed the Manhattan Project. Designing and building the bomb was such a complicated process that they employed more than 130,000 scientists and engineers. However, because it was so secret, hardly any of those involved understood exactly what was going on. Special laboratories and workshops were built at a remote location called Los Alamos in the American state of New Mexico. Local people were not told what the buildings were for, and staff working there were not allowed to discuss it with outsiders or even with colleagues in other parts of the site.

Because **the development of the bomb** was so important, everything possible was done to prevent any information leaking out of Los Alamos. Even the Russians weren't told what was going on, although they were on the same side in the war and were also fighting the Germans and Japanese. To keep it secret most of the scientists and engineers worked in very small teams on their own tiny piece of this enormously complex puzzle.

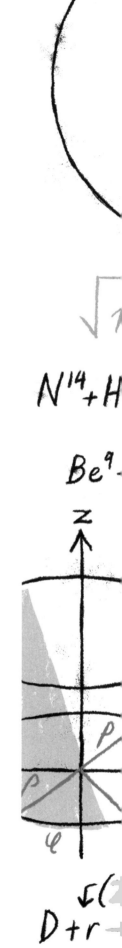

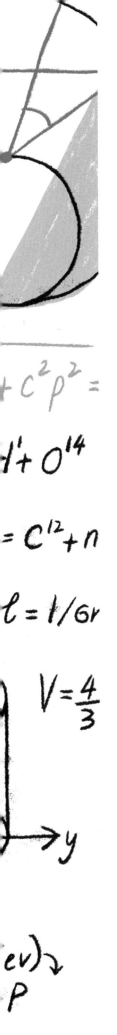

Only a few, very senior people knew how all these pieces fitted together and understood what the project was really about.

Eventually the teams working on the Manhattan Project won the race, but it cost more than \$2 billion to produce just two working bombs. Even this took so long to complete that by the time the bombs were ready, in August 1945, Germany had already surrendered. The Japanese were still fighting, however, and so the decision was taken to drop the bombs on two Japanese cities instead.

The effects of this were **even more awful** than anyone expected. Hiroshima and Nagasaki were completely destroyed in two gigantic explosions, and about 225,000 people lost their lives. Many people around the world found this genuinely horrifying, but less than a week later the Second World War was finally over.

Because the destruction of the two cities was so total, it is impossible even now to say precisely how many died in the ruins. Many people hoped there would be no more bombs of this sort, but soon afterwards the USSR began testing similar weapons of its own. British and American politicians were genuinely surprised to discover this and wondered how on earth the Russians had managed to work out how to build them.

The truth took some time to emerge. Because the race to build the first bomb had such high stakes, Los Alamos had been allowed to recruit several top scientists who had emigrated from Germany. Frisch and Peierls were both Jewish so they naturally wanted to defeat the country responsible for the murder of millions of Jews. But others had much more complicated reasons for joining the Manhattan Project and some of them couldn't be trusted. Klaus Fuchs was one of these.

Fuchs was born in Germany, but he had become a communist before escaping to England and qualifying as a theoretical physicist. His work was of such high quality that he had been invited to work with Peierls in Birmingham.

Unfortuately, as well as being a communist, Fuchs was a supporter of Stalin, the Soviet leader. Peierls didn't know it, but his colleague had already been in contact with staff at the Soviet Embassy in London. The Russians had arranged for Fuchs to meet one of their most experienced agents, a woman codenamed 'Sonya', who agreed to help him smuggle scientific secrets back to Moscow.

This meant that Fuchs had been spying on Peierls from the very start, but his big chance came when they moved to the US. Their research at Los Alamos was crucial to the success of the whole atomic project and Fuchs found

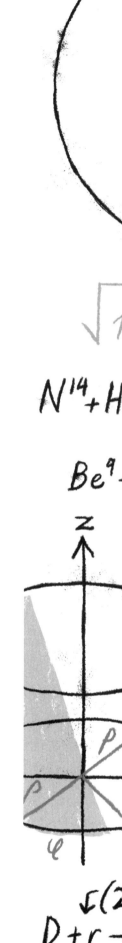

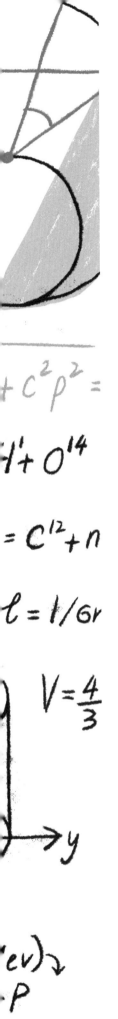

himself working closely with many of the most important nuclear engineers and scientists.

Fuchs believed that if the US was the only country with atomic weapons it would begin to dominate the world. He thought this would be bad for the future of communism, which is why he decided to send the Russians whatever documents and information he could get his hands on. It was this information that had enabled the USSR to build its own atomic bomb.

When the Russians tested the new weapon, it didn't take Britain or the US long to work out that they must have been helped by someone at Los Alamos. Fuchs was called in for questioning. At first he denied that he had done anything wrong, but then, after repeated interrogation, he confessed. He admitted he had been working for the Russians for several years and said he hadn't done it for money but because he thought it was the right thing to do.

Fuchs was convinced that the only thing that would stop the US dropping another bomb would be the risk of a counter-attack. He thought the fear of what we now call mutually assured destruction – an even more terrible third world war in which both sides would have nuclear weapons – was the best way to keep the peace between the US and the USSR.

His interrogators listened to his arguments and some of them may even have agreed with his theory. However, Fuchs had admitted spying on Britain, Canada and the US, and after a trial which lasted just ninety minutes he was sentenced to fourteen years in a British prison. During questioning he helpfully supplied MI6 with the names of several other Russian spies, but after he was released he left the country and, still claiming to be a communist, continued his research on behalf of the USSR.

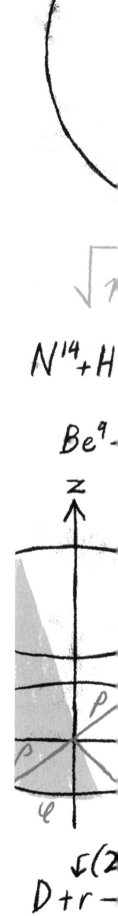

$+ c^2 p^2 =$

$4 + O^{14}$

$= C^{12} + n$

$\ell = 1/Gr$

$V = \dfrac{4}{3}$

$\longrightarrow y$

$ev) \searrow$

P

$n + 2H$

$r^2)(\sqrt{r}$

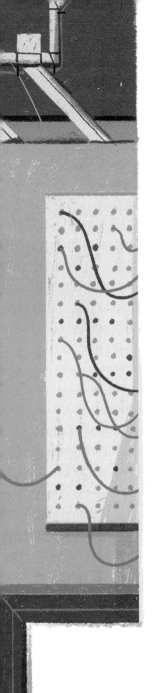

George Blake

The Secret Tunnel that Wasn't Secret

MI6 agent George Blake became a Russian spy after witnessing the terrible effects of American bombing raids on ordinary citizens during the Korean War.

The war had begun in 1950 when North Korea invaded South Korea, and it lasted for just over three years. The invasion was supported by two communist states, China and the USSR, while Britain and the US sided with South Korea. It wasn't as long or as terrible as the Second World War, but hundreds of thousands of troops were killed or wounded, and as many as three million civilians lost their lives.

Blake was captured by the North Korean forces and spent most of the war in various prison camps. Prisoners on both sides of the conflict were routinely beaten, tortured and starved, but Blake found the worst thing was seeing the effects of American air raids. He saw countless devastated villages as he was moved from one camp to the next and noticed that most of the dead in these small, rural communities were women and children, as the men were away fighting. Blake slowly began to feel he was on the wrong side.

As this feeling grew stronger, he secretly arranged a meeting with the guards at one of the camps in a place where they wouldn't be overheard. He told the startled guards that he worked for MI6, but that he now wanted to join the Russian secret service, the KGB. The KGB was delighted to recruit a British agent and arranged for him to be released so that he could return home and begin spying on Britain.

Back in London, Blake kept all this secret and carried on working at MI6. He even married one of the organisation's secretaries. Unknown to anyone else, the KGB had supplied him with a special, miniaturised Minox camera. Most cameras at this time were large and heavy, but this new one was sleek enough to hide in his trouser pocket. Blake used it to photograph a mass of secret documentation which passed through his office.

Blake arranged to meet a Russian contact every three weeks, when he would hand over the photographs. He took great care to cover his actions and make sure he wasn't followed, so no one at MI6 suspected him. Two years later he was given a new job and sent to Berlin.

In 1955 this was an important and incredibly exciting place for any spy. Ten years earlier the city had been divided in two after the defeat of Germany: the eastern half was still occupied by the USSR and the western half was controlled by Britain, France and the US. While ordinary Berliners tried to get on with their lives, agents on each side of the divide were constantly spying on each other and trying to collect information about what was going on in the other half of the city.

One of the most extraordinary examples of this was a daring scheme organised by the British and Americans to dig an underground tunnel linking their part of Berlin to the Russian sector. Equipment inside the tunnel was connected to East Berlin's main telephone cables so that MI6 and the CIA could record thousands of hours of Russian communications. The 450-metre-long tunnel cost several million dollars to excavate and equip, and was so secret that even the German authorities were not told about it. But George Blake knew about the plan and had informed his Russian superiors before work had even begun.

In Berlin Blake was supposed to be making contact with Russian spies and persuading them to spy for Britain: in other words, he was a double agent pretending to recruit other double agents. He had no intention of actually persuading anyone to spy for Britain, but his new role made it much easier for him to meet Russians than it had been in London. Even if someone from MI6 saw him talking to a Russian agent, they would just assume he was doing his job.

Blake's treachery meant that the expensive tunnel was already useless by the time it was completed. The Russians made sure that any secret telephone calls were made in code so that no one listening to them could understand what was being said. They also pretended not to notice when the tunnel was accidentally exposed the next winter by the heat of the equipment inside it melting the snow on the ground above.

The KGB kept silent about the tunnel's existence for almost a year. Blake was one of the Soviet Union's most valuable spies, and the KGB didn't want to lose him if the British or Americans realised their secret had been exposed and began to look for someone to blame.

Once Blake had left Berlin, the Russians pretended to discover the tunnel. Britain and the US were publicly accused of spying, which caused great embarrassment to the governments of both countries.

George Blake was later identified as a double agent and the source of the leak, and he was put on trial. As a committed communist, he admitted what he had done and said he did not think of himself as a criminal. Even when he was accused of betraying dozens of his fellow agents (some of whom had been killed as a result) he said he couldn't be sure about this because he had handed over so many thousands of secret documents that he couldn't remember what they were.

At the end of the trial Blake was sent to Wormwood Scrubs prison for forty-two years, which at the time was the longest sentence ever handed down by a British judge. Many people thought this was too harsh and so three of them decided to help him escape from prison. This turned out to be surprisingly easy: Blake used a homemade rope ladder to climb over the wall while the prison guards were watching a film. After being hidden in the back of an old camper van, he was driven back to East Germany.

George Blake eventually settled in Russia. He received a special KGB pension and lived there until his death in 2020 at the age of ninety-eight.

Zvi Aharoni

Tracking Down a Nazi

Spies don't just steal secrets. In March 1960 an Israeli agent travelled more than twelve thousand kilometres to South America in search of something much larger than a document or a photograph. His mission was to find an escaped war criminal and smuggle him out of the country to be put on trial.

Agents working for Mossad, Israel's secret service, had heard rumours that one of Adolf Hitler's most powerful officials was hiding out in Argentina. Several senior Nazi politicians and military leaders had gone on trial for war crimes after the regime's defeat in 1945, but many more had fled the country and changed their names to avoid detection. South America was a

particularly popular hiding place. It was a very long way from Europe, and governments there often refused to help find the missing men or to send them back when they were discovered.

One of the most notorious names on the list of wanted men was a fifty-four-year-old called Adolf Eichmann. During the war, Eichmann had been one of Germany's most important officials and a brilliant organiser, arranging the transportation of millions of Jews and others to their deaths in concentration camps. At the end of the war he had been captured by the US army, but managed to escape before anyone realised who he really was.

Mossad knew that many senior Nazis had made their way to South America, but to begin with no one believed the rumours about Eichmann being there. It took several months before Mossad agreed to send an agent to investigate. Eventually, Zvi Aharoni was sent to Argentina to check up on a man who called himself Ricardo Klement and worked for the Mercedes-Benz car company in the capital, Buenos Aires.

Aharoni's mission had to remain top secret because Argentina was one of the countries which refused to help track down Nazis. He was given a false passport and a special briefcase fitted with a hidden camera. He used this to photograph a seemingly ordinary house in a suburb of Buenos Aires which was thought to be Klement's new home.

A search through city documents quickly revealed that the house was actually owned by someone called Mrs Fichmann. Aharoni thought this must be a misprint for 'Mrs Eichmann', although it seemed odd that her husband should go to the trouble of changing his own name but not hers. To make absolutely sure, the agent went back to the house in the hope of getting close-up photographs of Eichmann without being discovered. He almost didn't manage this after accidentally crashing his rented car (and nearly losing the camera film), but once he had the photographs Aharoni was confident he had identified the right man.

After seeing Eichmann's photograph, the Israeli authorities decided very quickly to kidnap him. More than eighty thousand Germans lived in Buenos Aires (many of whom had supported Hitler) and the Argentinian government had shown no interest in pursuing foreign criminals. Because of this, it seemed highly unlikely that the country would agree to Eichmann being taken to Israel to stand trial.

A small task force of eight Mossad agents was hastily assembled and flown in secret to Buenos Aires. While some of them kept the house under surveillance, others went off to hire two large cars and to rent somewhere they could use as a safe house. The agents watching the house noticed that their target was a man of habit. 'Ricardo' caught the same bus

to work every day, and every evening it dropped him off close to his home just after half past seven. They decided that this would be the perfect time to snatch him off the street.

A couple of nights later the two rented cars drew up on the road. One was positioned close to Eichmann's house with its bonnet open, so it looked like it had broken down. The other was parked further away, its headlights pointing towards the bus stop so they would dazzle Eichmann slightly as he got off the bus. The men waited nervously as 7.30 came and went. At 7.40 there was still no sign of the bus. At ten to eight they began wondering if Eichmann had been tipped off about the ambush. Then, just as they were about to leave, the bus turned into the street and slowed as it neared the bus stop.

As the men watched, Eichmann stepped off the bus and began walking towards his front door. As he passed the car with its bonnet up, one of the Israelis called to him using the only Spanish words any of them knew – '*Un momento, Señor*' ('One moment, sir') – as if he needed help with the engine.

Their target hesitated and reached into his pocket. Eichmann probably wanted his door key but, fearing he had a gun, the other agents leapt on top of him. They wrestled him to the ground and within seconds had bundled Eichmann into the car, taped a gag over his

mouth and warned him that if he continued struggling or yelling he would be shot.

Back at the safe house, Aharoni explained who they were and why they were there. He then asked the prisoner to confirm his name. At first, the prisoner insisted he was Ricardo Klement, but then changed his mind and said his name was really Otto Henninger. No one believed this either and, when they asked a third time, he finally admitted he was SS-*Obersturmbannführer* Adolf Eichmann. He also told Aharoni that he was prepared to be tried in court, but only in Argentina or Germany. Aharoni told him the plan was to take him to Israel and Eichmann eventually agreed to go.

Aharoni still had to smuggle his captive out of Argentina without the authorities finding out, so more false documents were produced to make it look as though Eichmann worked for the Israeli airline, El Al. By midnight on 20 May 1960, less than three months after Aharoni's arrival in Argentina, Eichmann was on board a four-engined Bristol Britannia airliner flying high above the Atlantic Ocean.

By 1960 many countries were beginning to think there was no point in prosecuting anyone so long after the war, but Israel was determined to show that the guilty should pay for their crimes. Eichmann had demanded a fair trial before leaving Argentina, and Aharoni had promised him one. Now

Israel's government even agreed to pay a top German lawyer to defend him (something Germany refused to do) but everyone knew the case against Eichmann was a strong one.

Nearly one hundred Holocaust survivors were brought in to personally identify Eichmann and to testify against him. After a court case lasting an astonishing nine months, Eichmann was found guilty of multiple crimes against humanity and hanged. More than sixty years later, this is still the only death sentence ever passed by an Israeli court.

Zvi Aharoni wasn't in court to hear the verdict. After retiring he changed his name and moved to a small village in southern England. When he died in 2012, few if any villagers realised what an important role their ninety-one-year-old neighbour had played in bringing such a notorious criminal to justice.

Epilogue

The true stories in this book mostly relate to agents operating in Europe, and many of the dangerous missions described in it occurred during the Second World War or shortly after. Spies do a lot of important work all over the world when countries are at war with each other, but they are active in peacetime too. Secret agents have been around for hundreds of years (possibly even longer) because real spies aren't just interested in military secrets and sabotage. Often their jobs involve spying on businesses or politicians or on other important people in positions of power.

Organisations in many if not most countries have employed spies at some time, and a few governments employ thousands of them all the time. This is hardly a secret – organisations like MI5 and the CIA are famous and some even have their own websites – but governments rarely discuss their activities or admit that anyone working for them is really a spy.

For obvious reasons the men and women who do the actual spying have to stay quiet and hidden while they are working, but it's interesting that hardly any of them talk about it much afterwards either, even years and years after they have retired. Often they are forbidden to discuss this sort of thing with anyone, but sometimes they just don't want to.

This is certainly the case with the spies in this book, even though most of them would have been welcomed home as heroes had anyone known what they had done. A lot of former agents wouldn't even agree to be interviewed, let alone write a book or go into a television or radio studio to describe missions they had planned or taken part in.

There are many reasons for this. Even the bravest agent could be genuinely shy or modest about his or her achievements. The best spies are rarely the sort of people who like to draw attention to themselves in the way James Bond does, and several people described in these pages actually refused to accept the medals they were offered, or took them and put them away in a drawer instead of showing them off to their friends and families.

Others perhaps just wanted to get on with their lives. Even if they didn't want to forget about the war, they must have welcomed the opportunity to go back to being an ordinary person again after living

such a strange life for so many years. It's also possible that some of the agents had trouble adjusting to a more normal existence after the dangers and excitement of war. These are the ones who suffered from what we now call PTSD (post-traumatic stress disorder) as a result of the terrible things they had experienced, such as knowing friends and comrades had been tortured and even killed.

Reasons like these go a long way to explaining why few spies become famous, even in old age. Unfortunately it also means that, as we rarely find out who they are, even the bravest, most successful ones don't always get the thanks or the respect they deserve. Indeed, sometimes the only ones we do hear about are the enemy spies who get caught or the traitors and double agents who betray their own countries, often for money rather than something they genuinely believe in.

Most of the people in this book were genuinely heroic, however, and they deserve our respect and thanks even if they were happy to be left in peace once they had retired. These men and women risked their lives every day, and many of them did so from an astonishingly young age. They may have done what they did to serve their own country, or to free another country from enemy occupation, or because they could see a way to save the lives of innocent men, women and children. In a few cases this meant saving the lives of hundreds or even thousands, and of course often it led to the death of the agent at the hands of the enemy.

Sadly, none of the heroes in this book are still alive today, but it is important that we remember them for their bravery and the extraordinary things that they accomplished. To help us to do this there are several memorials, in Britain as well as at some of those terrible places abroad where agents are known to have been imprisoned or killed.

One of the newest is **a striking bronze sculpture** situated very close to the MI6 headquarters, overlooking the Thames at Vauxhall in London. The memorial is a bust of a courageous agent called Violette Szabo who lived nearby and it commemorates the incredible heroism of all the men and women of the wartime Special Operations Executive.

Many of the people working in the building walk past it every day, and any one of them could be a real, live secret agent, although you would never know. If you visit this part of London and see the memorial, stop and think for a moment about the people it honours. They were remarkable individuals, and all of us have a lot to thank them for.